D1808162

9780719521485

FIRST PERSON SINGULAR

Hubert van Zeller is a Benedictine monk, a distinguished author, and sculptor. He has written this book in the first person singular to preserve the singularity of his own point of view, and because he feels that while a writer may not always know what is going on in other people's heads, he ought to know what is going on in his own.

In a rich and varied collection of sketches, in which fact is sometimes cloaked in fiction, his experiences fall into four distinct categories: childhood and youth spent among relatives of distinguished, and in the case of great-uncles and aunts, idiosyncratic temperament; pilgrimages and retreats – on which the sacred is delightfully tinged with more profane misadventures; America seen with an enthusiastic and keenly observant eye; and a final section on Wales.

First Person Singular

HUBERT VAN ZELLER

JOHN MURRAY

To GERVASE

©Hubert van Zeller 1970

All rights reserved. No part of this publication
may be reproduced, stored in a retrieval system,
or transmitted, in any form or by any means,
electronic, mechanical, photocopying, recording or
otherwise, without the prior permission of John
Murray (Publishers) Ltd., 50 Albemarle Street,
London, W1X 4BD.

Printed in Great Britain by
Lewis Reprints Ltd,
Port Talbot, Glamorgan.

0 7195 2148 3

'I hold it a noble task to rescue from oblivion those who deserve to be eternally remembered.'
Pliny

'It is essential to the sanity of mankind that everyone should think everyone else is crazy.'
Emily Dickinson

CONTENTS

Acknowledgements are due to *Good Housekeeping* in which PORTRAIT OF AN ANGRY MAN, first appeared; to *Blackwood's Magazine* for ON THE HOUSE; to *Woman's Realm* for STELLA; to *The Cornhill Magazine* for ISN'T THIS WHERE WE CAME IN?, WATERS OF THE MISSISSIPPI DEEP AND STRONG, BED AND BREAKFAST and LOCAL TIME.

FAMILY

TRAPPERS TRAPPED

I was a born nephew. Unlike sisters, aunts do not climb trees or slide on ice; but although my lack of interest in these pursuits may have been influenced by aunt-preponderance, I know now I would have been in any case out of my element as climber, slider, tobogganer, somersaulter, splasher, or mud-pie roller and thrower. From the age of six until I became a conforming cog in the public-school machine — and perhaps beyond this climacteric — I was a prig. Not a whole-time prig; just a prig when people were looking. There were occasions when I deliberately suspended the role, as when, in a mood of ill-mannered levity, I held up a bowl of ice-cream to an electric fan and enjoyed seeing the spatter of white flaking my own and other people's Harris tweeds, but I cannot help feeling that in the part of naughty boy I was acting out of character. I was type-cast as the little fellow who was never rough. Why then should I suddenly have turned trapper?

In the house next door lived a boy who bore the unlikely Christian name of Bridge. Bridge could be depended upon for roughness, especially at parties. We did not care for one another much, Bridge and I, but were thrown together because we were neighbours. Bridge was nine to my eight, so I had always to defer. I was ready enough to defer. For one thing he embodied an Englishness which made me aware of (not ashamed of but aware of) my continental ancestry. There was very little up-guards-and-at-'em about me. Though my attitude towards him was devoid of hero-worship I recognised in him the eternal gangster. Something which I was not. He the enviable crook, the adventurer, the buccaneer: I the man who trips up over the fuse-wire. But even so there was a certain aura about our joint undertakings, and when initiated into the mysteries of trapping I felt I had graduated from the play-pen to the prairie.

The trapper's technique has probably been developed since those simple idyllic days. I can write only of what I know. At the turn of the century one still lurked behind a hedge, spotting. It did not seem greatly to matter whether one spotted birds, rabbits, squirrels, mice or even ants. The important thing was to spot, and, having spotted, to entice and then to slay. The instrument devised for our trapping showed nothing of the tooth-and-spring cruelty, which in any case would not have worked with ants, but there was little refinement in its effect. Bridge, the master mind, would strap a tennis racquet to a long pole which would be pushed through the bushes into a clearing. I would be allowed to spread fronds of fern over the pole. On the flat of the tennis racquet Bridge would place a rusty metal tray (a plate would have caught the eye of whatever animal happened to be watching the preparations for its death), and on to the tray he would pour a cupful of warm glue. Nuts soaked in bacon fat would then be sprinkled over the glue, and back we would nip behind our hedge. It was then that the interminable spotting began. Today a computer might be able to cut down the time wasted by the spotter, but in the more leisurely age before the First War one waited and waited for quarry to come along. That quarry ever came along at all, the concoction being as disagreeable as it was, is surprising, but come it did, and though I was bored to distraction at having to wait for something to happen I was sickened when something did.

If Bridge sensed my disgust he never taunted me with it, and I knew better than to mention it. In bed at night the picture of paws, tails, claws pulling desperately away from the glue assumed a particularly unpleasant character, and I would wonder too at the morality of the trapping business. What surprises me today is that I did not consult my parents on this point. I must have argued, with the completely fallacious reasoning which we adopt right through life, that what was all right for Bridge must be all right also for me. Or perhaps I assumed that misgivings of this sort were just what a 'weedy' boy might be expected to feel, and that the solution lay not in being more ethical but in being less weedy.

I remember one other thing, a more engaging thing than that already described, about my companion in crime. On the approach of prey, whether fur or feather, Bridge would whisper in my ear the words 'Unless my senses deceive me' . . . and then he would let me know what his keen hunter's eye had spied. For some reason I found

11

this very funny (and still do), yet when I tried it on at home it was not thought to be funny in the least. After a while, since it not only failed to amuse but positively exasperated, I ceased to use the formula. Families evidently have their own idiom, and if you employ a different idiom you are a copy-cat. Seeing that the whole of education rests on the copy-cat principle, there is a confusion here which has since struck me as peculiar.

The trapping phase did not last long. Bridge went to one school; I, a year later, to another. Bridge's family left that part of the country, and so did mine. So it must have been a full eight years before we met again. Bridge, his mother, and his sister Joanie (the father, a much decorated colonel, had been treacherously killed while concluding peace negotiations between warring tribes) were living in Bedford. I was at my Aunt Berthe's in Lower Belgrave Street. During the summer holidays I was urged by my father, who kept up with people and who liked everyone to meet everyone else on every possible occasion, to take a train to Bedford and 'see how your old friend Bridge is getting on'. My mother, perhaps aware of an influence which I had not myself recognised at the time, was less enthusiastic. 'His old friend Bridge,' she suggested, 'has got on without him for years . . . I don't see why he shouldn't go on getting on without him.'

'Well Joanie and their mother then,' my father insisted, 'they would love the boy to come.' I doubted this, but it was less trouble to go than to argue. So I went.

In the train my feelings swung from lively excitement to dire foreboding. I was sixteen, so Bridge would be seventeen. Joanie would be even older, nearly nineteen. I tried to remember everything I could about them; all the wrong pictures kept flitting through my mind. From my memories of Bridge aged nine, the swashbuckling leader, I pieced together Bridge the captain of the eleven, the prefect whose cry of 'fag' brought a scurry of eager frightened feet, the cadet officer in the O.T.C. with his Sam Browne gleaming in the sun, the athlete on prize-day collecting an armful of silver cups. I wondered too how he was at this moment reconstructing, from his memories, me. The fear that I was still weedy beyond redemption drove me to the looking-glass in the railway carriage: I surveyed as much of myself as the rectangle above the cushions allowed. What I saw was

12

less than reassuring. I was not even quite sure, though my father had supervised this feature of the expedition, about my clothes. Bowler hat, kid gloves, grey flannel suit, modest socks and tie, unemphatic shoes. Correct enough in my father's eyes, but how would all this appear to Bridge the 'blood' and (though this did not matter so much) to Joanie the recent 'flapper'?

I need not have worried. At Bedford awaiting me on the platform was a Bridge whom I had not envisaged. For one thing he was an inch or two shorter than I was, and for another, unless my senses deceived me, he was wearing a school cap. Not weedy by any count, but nevertheless, not the caveman whom I recalled gaily dismembering rabbits, whistling happily while disembowelling thrushes. Suddenly I saw him, and I felt guilty at seeing him so, as mixing chemicals at the back of the chemist's shop, as casting accounts in the ledger while seated on a high stool, as kneeling on one knee with pins in his mouth and a flat sliver of chalk in one hand while the other hand plucks at a temporary stitching.

It was a terrible day. Joanie flashed in and out of the house, telephoning and changing her clothes, turning on the gramophone and turning it off, dismissing me as 'sweet in that funny bowler you all wear now'. Bridge did his best as host, offering me a cigarette and smoking one selfconsciously himself, but the performance lacked conviction. Their mother tinkled away with the tea things and repetitive observations about the old days, repetitive questions about the new days, and repetitive laments about the time in between. Only for one brief moment did the past come back, and this was when, left to ourselves 'to compare notes about your respective schools', Bridge tried to tell me a funny story. A dirty story. He must have seen me wince, and just for a flash have recognised his one-time lieutenant, for he said, more to himself than to me, 'Same old prude I see.'

Moral: whether you step out of your element or into it, whether you are paw or hoof or pad or foot, you get stuck. All the world a stage? It is nothing of the sort. It is a trap.

13

THE GIRLS

Charlotte and Victoria, the girls, were sisters. Charlotte must have been the elder because she was always mentioned first, but the question of seniority was not one upon which I speculated. I must have been about six when I was taken to see them, and they, with perhaps three years between their ages, would have been getting on for seventy. They shared a house in London, in Chelsea, from which one could see the river and hear such Thames noises as hootings, whistles, sirens, and fog-horns. The house was tall and narrow, like themselves, and everything in it was of such frailty that one moved with caution. Everyone in my family called them 'the girls', even in front of us children, because a brother of theirs, a generation or two earlier, had referred to them as such. 'Isn't it about time some of us went to see the girls?' my father would ask one day at breakfast. 'No,' my mother would reply. A few days later the suggestion would, reluctantly, be repeated. A dutiful aunt would say, 'I suppose so,' and another dutiful aunt would say, 'I'll let them know beforehand.' The girls did not like being caught on the hop.

Had we taken the trouble to get to know them better, the girls might have counted as belonging to the family — one of their brothers having married one of my aunts — but they never qualified. It was clear to me, certainly by the time I was seven and had been to see them on a number of occasions, that they lived in a different world. It was not a question of money or class, for as regards these things there was nothing in it, nor could politics or religion have accounted for it. I once asked my father, after a particularly unmixing tea party, whether perhaps the girls did not care for children. 'I doubt if they've thought about it,' said my father; but he knew what I meant because he added: 'The whole sniff of the place is different, don't you see?'

Looking back I can see that the girls crystallised at some point and thereafter remained as though suspended from one of their own chandeliers. Slender, transparent, sometimes reflecting a shaft of

14

sunlight, tinkling discreetly and pleasantly at the least movement, but for ever set and in outline clearly defined. When an opinion was required from either of them, it was jointly voiced. Their instinctive reflexes were, as were their clothes which I shall come to in a minute, predictable. Even at the time I must have been old enough to distinguish between extending hospitality and imparting it, because the impression I formed was that of duty rather than of enjoyment. This was doubtless why our approach had to be heralded beforehand: only partly to give the sisters time to get in the white-enamelled Fuller's cake with the walnut knobs; more especially to give the role of hostess its psychological *montage*. Once addressed to a situation, Miss Charlotte and Miss Victoria could be depended upon to make a go of it. But no address, no go.

Small-boned, straight-backed, rigid in their creaking frames of whale and steel, these elderly spinster ladies made no concessions either to comfort or fashion. Ankle-length dresses of black rustling material and identical cut, close-fitting silk bodices, also black, buttoning high to the neck, long sleeves, open-work black mittens into the right-hand palm of which was tucked a very small and purely ceremonial lace handkerchief. Never shoes, always boots. But boots of such a delicate texture as to dismiss at once comparison with *real* boots. How far up the leg they reached, these boots, one would of course never know, but whether buttoned or laced (the elastic-sided were a slipshod boot and on that score ruled out), they were not of a kind to be seen in shop windows. On each head the grey hair, parted in the middle, was swept high off the forehead till it reached a flat, made-up velvet bow, which in turn was surmounted by a firm round bun. No make-up (this was before the First World War), no earrings or other rings, no bracelets. Pince-nez on a thin silver chain would hardly be considered jewellery, nor would a watch hanging from a shining black belt on a broad ribbon of strong watered silk. The sole adornment for adornment's sake was a rather large cameo brooch, oval and curved: from one throat rose Diana standing in her chariot, quiver on shoulder and bow slung across the body; from the other blind and bearded Oedipus leaning in an agony of self-reproach upon a staff (or it may have been Neptune, for he wore a sort of fireman's helmet). These cameos proclaimed to me a background of classical learning the

15

existence of which, as I grew older, I came to doubt. Less and less could I see Miss Charlotte and Miss Victoria wandering in some leafy grove of Academia, breasting the clouds that rolled down the slopes of Olympus. Those narrow feet of theirs were made to tread the floors of Pontings and Whiteley's, and perhaps, on occasions of planned excursion, the sandy paths of Kew. But the girls did not often stray far from base. Sometimes the three of us would get as far as Kensington Gardens and the Park: they sitting poker-erect and silent on the hard green chairs supplied by the corporation, I, hardly more voluble, feeding the ducks or sailing my boat.

No, the sisters were not of a literary turn of mind. The world of ideas too, of definition and abstract speculation, seemed closed to them. One wonders if there was any positive cerebration at all. Polite accomplishment was more in their line, but even here the creative gift was far from active. On arriving at their house for tea — let in by the parlourmaid Parker (whose name was Moira Noonan), who took my father's hat as though it were the papal tiara — we would mount the stairs to the drawing-room, which was on the first floor, and hear ourselves announced in a rehearsed voice. Our names would be greeted with little yelps of surprise and delight, and we would be shown in. The stage had been set since luncheon. As there were no canaries or goldfish — pets popular at that time among maiden ladies ('There wouldn't be room for them anyway,' was my mother's comment, 'thank God') — our hostesses could receive us without the distraction of competition. There they would be, each discovered at her task. Miss Charlotte was usually engaged in needlework or crochet-work which would one day form a fringe to an altar cloth. Miss Victoria would be sorting out sepia prints showing the more frequented parts of India, Egypt, and other lands where her younger brother Robert had served as colonel of his regiment. These faded and curling photographs, in every way suggesting autumn leaves, were meant one day to be stuck upon the thick cardboard pages of an album which now lay in Miss Victoria's lap. But whether because there was no gum, or because once gummed they would leave Miss Victoria with nothing else to do, the day of gumming never dawned. Certainly whenever we came to tea the scene was the same: needlework being smoothed out on one pair of knees, the album being lifted from another. While the grown-up visitors were exclaiming at the intricacy of the needlework, I would steer my way through the room's hazards to see how far the photographs had got. Gibraltar 1892 . . . Barbados 1895. The album's heavy pages were bevelled and gilded, and across its padded green cover was printed in bold lettering of gold, in case one might mistake its purpose, the word *Photographs*.

The tea ritual was invariable. Spirit-lamp under the hot water; silver dish-covers over plates of buttered toast, muffins, crumpets, hot teacake; tomato sandwiches, cucumber sandwiches, potted-meat sandwiches; the Fuller's cake on the lowest tier of the cake-stand — the implication being that, as a delicacy and still more as a *bought* delicacy, it was to be approached last — and enamel-handled knives and forks to eat it with. There was a silver bowl with slices of lemon for the China tea, and a great many other silver bowls besides. My mother used to annoy the girls, though they tried not to show it, by tipping the tongs out of the sugar-bowl and taking the lumps with her fingers. She also refused to use the soft lace-bordered napkins which to me spelled elegance and distinction but to her were symbols of the hill station. Though they were fond of my father, and I have never known a woman who was not, the girls disapproved, I imagine, of my mother's chic. When my father had finished eating almost all the cake, and my mother had wiped her mouth with deliberation on his handkerchief, and my aunts were beginning to sag after too many cups of tea, Miss Charlotte would pop the snuffer over the flame of the spirit-lamp and pronounce the formula for which we had been waiting: 'If you wouldn't mind pulling the bell, Victoria, then Parker can come in and clear.' In would come Moira Noonan, the tea things would be cleared, female cheeks would briefly meet, my father would bow and kiss the tips of each hostess's right hand, and I, feeling extremely foolish, would imitate the action. Then the trooping downstairs to the hall: umbrellas for the aunts, top-hat and gloves for my father, muff for my mother, flat corduroy cap with a button on the top for me — the cap to match the corduroy leggings of which I was inordinately proud and which I wore whenever possible with my knickerbocker suit — and out through the fog we would go to my grandmother's waiting brougham. If there were more than one aunt present it would be a tight squeeze, and we would all wave at the two dark figures standing at the long window and outlined against the gaslit room behind them.

Then came 1914 and the war. In the cause of patriotism and austerity the three maids were replaced by charladies who came in at odd times and who added considerably to household expenses. These I remember as George Belcher characters: squashed straw hats decorated with cherries, fingers showing through the ends of worn gloves, shawls, string bags, falling hairpins, and no inhibitions here about elastic-sided boots. Uncertain though their labours were, the charladies eased the lot of Miss Charlotte and Miss Victoria who in all probability had never made a bed in their lives or laid a table. The economies did not extend to the kitchen, so cook remained throughout the war and seemed not to repine at the depletion of the domestic staff. Being now at school I saw less of the girls than hitherto. Also I was given to understand at home that they would rather one did not visit them. This puzzled me. Was it on account of the war that they were not seeing people? Poverty? Old age? Experience of my family had taught me that if I asked questions I would be told nothing, but that if I waited long enough the story would filter through. The first hint took the form of: 'It's not about him I mind particularly . . . but it must be so awful for the girls.' A few weeks later, and from a different aunt: 'They feel it very much, poor things, and I can't think why because it's not as if he was in and out all day.' Thus far it might have been a death or a sickness. But who was 'he'? If everything had been above board the information would have been shared with me. So I concluded, correctly, that something was below board.

From more precise references it emerged that a younger brother (not, fortunately, Robert, the one who had married my aunt) was in prison. He was the baby of that family, a widower and nearly sixty, and apparently had always been spoilt. Now he had disgraced himself, had been sentenced to eighteen months, had had his name in all the papers except the Catholic ones, and had sent his two elder sisters into self-imposed seclusion. I could remember Clarence, having once seen him through the banisters on the occasion of a dinner party. A sad, drooping figure in white tie and tails, not at all suggestive of villainous intent. Try as I might to invest this kinsman-by-marriage with the glamour of crime, I found a flaccid, heavily moustached face

18

getting in the way. What could such a one have done to earn the ball and chain which I associated with his present state? I decided to suspend my normal procedure, and ask. I felt, again as it happens correctly, that my schoolboy acquaintance with the literature of violence might in this instance prove misleading, and though at the back of my mind I still hoped to hear that Uncle Clarence had cracked a safe or been involved in a train hold-up I sensed a gap between aura and actuality. So when next I heard my elders expressing sorrow for the girls, I put it to them that since part of the matter was already known to me I might be allowed to know the rest.

'It was nothing very terrible, dear,' said my Aunt Yolande, who was the aunt to be counted on in these questions of subtlety, 'at least not one of those nasty things one reads about.' Which disposed of *that* doubt anyway. Questioned further she elaborated slightly: 'I believe it was something to do with stocks and shares, which are muddling enough at the best of times, and those big loans which people have in the City.'

'It was a mistake his ever joining the City,' said Aunt Berthe, 'he was never any good at sums.'

'He was dashed good at sums if you want to know,' said my father who was reading the paper and who I thought had not been listening, 'and only just not dashed good enough.' Yolande irritated my father, who judged her vapid manner and idiom to be affectations, which they were not. Berthe irritated him too, but he got on better with her because she did not crumple up. I am afraid he rather enjoyed crumpling Yolande up. 'If pinching people's cash isn't one of those nasty things,' he said, going back to his paper, 'I'd like to know what is.'

By the time Clarence came out it was too late. Our efforts to get in touch again with Miss Charlotte and Miss Victoria were met with affectionately couched evasions. The war was over now, so perhaps they would live abroad. They did not in fact go abroad, but stayed on in the Chelsea house with their crochet and sepia photographs. And then I suppose they died.

ACCORDING TO MY GRANDMOTHER

Like all autocrats my grandmother both made and broke her own laws. Also there were laws for her children, and laws, much milder ones I am glad to say, for her grandchildren. Guests had to conform. She would not allow breakfast in bed, newspapers at the breakfast-table, a fire in one's room before a certain hour. While coats and hats had to be hung up in a little room off the hall, toys might be found almost anywhere except in the dining-room and in the two very formal drawing-rooms. Nicknames were discouraged — though she herself had a nickname for everybody — and the use of slang was severely frowned upon. While her own conversation never got within hailing distance of slang, she reserved to herself the right of judging between what was and what was not a slang term.

One of her rulings which annoyed everyone was that neither salt, pepper nor mustard might appear on the table. 'They know down-stairs exactly how much to put in the food,' she held, 'and to add more is to insult the chef. Besides the dining-room is not the place where you do your cooking.' We all knew she was not above insulting the chef if she had a mind to, and that she greatly enjoyed mixing a salad in the dining-room. This she performed at a sideboard, very expertly and with everyone standing round so that all might learn and in turn pass on the charisma to their own families. Salt, pepper, mustard, and goodness knows what else were used without stint. Apart from the salad, the idea of the ban must have been something she had inherited from her mother or grandmother, because when she died and the silver was shared out among her children, the pepper-pots, salt-cellars and mustard-pots, all bearing either the Halwyll or de Seigneux crest, were as good as new while the other pieces bore marks of years of polishing and wear. The only person who was allowed to make salads in her presence was Rita, who, of her nine children, was assumed to be favourite. This preference, however, could be in abeyance during a row. If the row were a

20

particularly splendid one, favour of any sort would be suspended for days and sometimes weeks.

Few people of my acquaintance, either at the time of which I write or since, have possessed to so marked a degree the power of creating, and then of maintaining, a feud. My grandmother made it a point of honour to put others in the wrong. Only once have I seen her stumped. The occasion has remained in my memory because not only was she then at a loss, a rare enough phenomenon, but also because in this instance she bore no malice. Mildred, Rita's daughter and my cousin, was admittedly one of the privileged, but when this twelve-year-old said of a guest who had been to tea that he reminded her, on account of his shuffling gait and squeaky voice, of an Eskimo, the licence extended to the young was felt to be strained. Instead of the expected explosion there was silence: a silence broken only by Mildred's amplification '. . . an *old* Eskimo'. My grandmother, roused at last and feeling it her duty to shut Mildred up, said icily: 'I would like to know when was the last time you saw an Eskimo — an old Eskimo.' 'Do you mean alive or dead?' was Mildred's instant response.

From my grandmother I learned, perhaps unfortunately as things turned out, to appreciate grandeur. Grandeur takes many forms; my grandmother and I responded to them all. While the rest of the family preferred comfort — innumerable towels warming away in the bathroom, unnecessary pillows piled high on every bed, sherry and biscuits more or less on call, fashionable magazines lying about everywhere — she and I plumped for the noble setting. Noble settings can be uncomfortable, can be ostentatious, can mask all sorts of insufficiencies, but they certainly provide satisfactions not reached by mere luxury. My grandmother would have been content to let the fire go out so long as she could see swans on a lake which she could call, however temporarily, her own. I would have been content to sleep in a dilapidated ballroom, and on the floor with moss pushing up between the boards, so long as I could project myself into a scene of vanished elegance. Indulging her taste (and mine) my grandmother used to rent each summer a country house which was felt by her more critical and less affluent relatives to be just a little beyond her place in English society. I have always cherished the idea that words

21

such as 'court' and 'hall' and 'park' held for her an especial appeal. Year after year the family would be established from June until September in a mansion – never the same for two years running – which bore an impressive address. Appearance mattered too, as already suggested, but not, apparently, plumbing. I possess a list of the houses rented by her between 1890 and 1912, and am always hoping for an excuse to visit some of them, paying at the door, to see if the magic still lingers. Those which I was old enough to take in are fused by memory into one, and I see, as though in a photograph out of focus, a single lofty pile of venerable but mixed design. In what wall was set that oriel window through which I waved at the postman coming up the drive? From what roof, forbidden to the climber, sprang those barley-sugar chimneys? Am I remembering or merely guessing at lily ponds, croquet lawns, rose gardens, stables of pink brick, topiary enclosures? It would seem that eye and mind are joined in a conspiracy to get things wrong, and so give to imagination – that restless handmaid always unreliable – an occasion for showing off.

Certainly there was little grandeur – and no occasion for showing off – about the house which my mother and father took in Alexandria and where I spent much of my boyhood when not in England. It was a semi-detached house with, from the architectural point of view, scarcely a redeeming feature. When shown a photograph of it, taken from the garden, my grandmother's only comment was, 'I'm sure the wallpaper is very pretty.' Nothing is so durable as a family dictum, and when I visited my aunt Yolande in hospital more than half a century after the observation was made, and asked her if she was feeling all right, her answer was, 'No, but I like the wallpaper.' The walls of her hospital room were of clinical white enamel.

In the way that the houses my grandmother took have become a composite house, the guests who used to come to stay have become a composite guest. This is odd, because her friends were mostly writers and painters – people less ready than most to merge into a haze of conformity. But perhaps it was the habit of poets and artists at that time to make themselves look as much as possible like men of business and industry. Perhaps in order to introduce a little more colour into her circle, which at one time or another included such supposedly colourful figures as Sarah Bernhardt, Oscar Wilde, Louis

Berton, Bret Harte (who spent the last years of his life in whatever house she happened to be living in and who died in her London house), my grandmother began to get interested in Buffalo Bill who was then performing in a circus. I doubt if her lasso ever roped Colonel Cody into her *salon* in Lancaster Gate, but I remember very vividly being taken to see the act and how I was told to shake hands nicely with the brave man who had killed so many redskins.

Few exercises are at once more fascinating and more futile than trying to trace the influences upon one's character. How far is a person the captive as well as the child of his genes? Looking back I see myself as an untidy mixture of my van Zeller father and my van de Velde grandmother. Both stood for order and discipline, but where my father went by the book my grandmother only quoted it. Yet although he was wedded to the laws which governed his course of action in the domestic field, my father took great exception to the insular mentality which refused to conform to the rituals of another land. 'It's a question of environment. Whatever your own habits you should not make yourself conspicuous by disregarding the habits of other people. Abroad you adapt yourself. If you go to Japan, for instance, you must remember not to cross your legs except in hotels and railway carriages.' I made a note of it. 'When in America you must learn to use the fork a lot more than we do in England. The knife is used only for cutting, which is reasonable enough after all, and when it has finished cutting, it is placed to one side and you go ahead with the fork in the right hand. The whole point of courtesy is that it considers the feelings of others. It would not be a mark of respect to kiss the hand of the gardener's wife when taking tea at the lodge because to be gallant beyond a certain point is to be insulting. Also it would be a piece of showing off.'

'What about the French custom which I've seen on the cinema,' I asked, 'do I have to kiss people on both cheeks when I'm in France?'

'No, you don't,' was the emphatic reply.

The prejudice against demonstrations of affection must have come from the way in which his own boyhood had been directed. Display of sentiment was, under his Dutch-Germanic papa, reduced to the minimum. When presenting himself each evening to wish his parents goodnight, he had been required to stand rigidly to attention with the middle finger pressed against the seam of his trousers. My mother and I, who had often heard him tell this, would extract an assurance when he returned from some ceremonial function that at the right moment his second finger had pointed stiffly down the *Hosennaht*.

When I think of my father's childhood I marvel that my own was not stricter. If I can remember the different degrees of mourning which we observed fifty years ago — at the age of eight I wore a black crepe band round my arm for the thirty days following my grand-mother's death — I wonder at the mildness of the code of bereavement when compared with the restrictions of an earlier generation. Mention of mourning recalls an observance which, whether of general accept-ance or simply another rule of his own, relates to my father's rule about Christmas cards. It seems that within the year of someone's death, Christmas cards were not sent or acknowledged. This was easy enough to practise when there had been a loss in one's own family, but how could one be expected to remember if one's friends had lost a relative within the past twelve months? Certainly the implication that the beginning of Christianity must take second place to private affairs is unfortunate.

The perfectionist is laughed at today. My father would not have laughed at the perfectionist because he was one. But though a purist, he was not I think a puritan. You might say of him that he was narrow in the licence he allowed, but not that he was prim. Anyway, standing six foot two and weighing some fifteen stone, he did not *look* prim. He would have held, quite rightly, that licence corrupts and that absolute licence corrupts absolutely. Just as he would have held it to be bad taste in painting and writing to be flamboyant. Affectation in art he abominated. He could not abide the work of Aubrey Beardsley. 'You can tell at once the chap's a bounder.' Though himself inclined to eccentricity he was the enemy of the mannered. To him the mannered was identified with the effeminate.

As a pendant to the above it may be worth recording that one of the few epigrams I ever heard him make was when he was lecturing me on the evil of artificial flowers. 'The whole point of a flower is that it is going to fade in a minute and you have to catch it before it does. These damn things — ' rattling the vase which stood between us — 'are Dorian Grays.'

24

In conclusion it is with some satisfaction that I note how insipid some of today's shibboleths, fabricated *by* the fabricated *for* the fabricated, would have seemed to my father. There had to be grounds for the legislation he imposed. Contrived the strictures may have been, but never wholly arbitrary.

So it was that his mind worked, ranging from the important to the trivial but always according to a system. The system attached a stigma to such things as getting a divorce, going back on a promise, cheating at cards, being cruel to animals. But it also attached a stigma to keeping people waiting, biting one's nails, not answering letters, folding up one's napkin at the end of the meal when dining out ('You should always leave it crumpled on the table because to fold it looks as though you expected it to be used again before it's sent to the wash'). It is strange that I, who from my earliest youth have seen my father's idiosyncratic foibles with a clear eye, should fall into the same trap — namely that of hedging myself about with rules which, though of a quite different order from his, seem designed to make life more and more complicated, nastier and nastier. Some atavistic urge, one must suppose, in both of us.

From both sides of the family I have inherited a respect for meticulous detail, but from only one side the tenacity which preserves fidelity from being nullified by exceptions. Enough has been said about the working of my grandmother's mind, but an incident which shows the working of my father's mind will bring out both similarity and the contrast. At the age of seventeen or so I was taking a glass of wine before luncheon when my father walked into the room. 'Is that sherry you're drinking?' he asked. 'Yes,' I replied, 'do you mind? I thought I was now at an age when —' 'I don't mind a bit your drinking sherry at any time of the day or night,' he said, 'but I see you are doing it out of a port glass. And apart from anything else, it's bad for the servants.' My grandmother, just as strict about the code but less logical when it came to a question of convenience, would have gladly taken her China tea out of a toothglass.

GREAT-UNCLES GALORE

Perhaps in a portrait gallery of the period they might not, either collectively or individually, have amounted to much, but from this distance my great-uncles seem to have been designed by a kindly providence for the character actor if not for the caricaturist. What is referred to today as the state of psychic contagion in which our lives are cast may be having the effect of eliminating all but the most advanced idiosyncratics. In an earlier and more spacious age, when their psyches were less adjacent, people developed their own potential (another modern term) as they went along, and ended up sharply distinct from their fellows. Without cultivating singularity, indeed believing themselves to be conformists, Victorians and Edwardians seem to have been richer in eccentricity than we are. Be this as it may, I would back the elders of my own family, great-uncle for great-uncle against any among the ancients now living in middle-class retirement up and down England's green and welfare land.

The youngest of my grandfather's brothers, Etienne, was a bachelor and more talkative than the others who were men of deep, almost morose, silence. He wore a toupé which, though fitting snugly enough, was darker and browner than the greying hair at the back and side, giving the effect of a chocolate sundae. He greatly disliked the Germans, his Gallican prejudice taking the form of punctuating his English with mock Germanic terms of his own making, which, with the accompanying accent, was thought to be very droll. Thus his umbrella became 'umgebrellenwerk', gooseberries were 'goosengoggen', and his hats were either the 'cylindersilkenhoot' or, if it were a bowler, the 'kammerpothoot'. He was a jolly man, spry and nimble on the feet as was shown by an occasional *pas seul* which was performed in kindly spirit for the entertainment of the young. It speaks well for his toupé that even in the swiftest gyration it never, to our disappointment, turned a hair. Great-uncle Etienne was less frequently a guest at my grandparents' house-parties than everyone would have wished. Without a wife he was wedded to his cigar, and since my grandmother allowed smoking only out of doors or in the room set aside for it, he preferred to stay at home. Like many of that time, he was given to practical jokes, but about these, since our tastes lie far apart, I cannot bring myself to write. In fairness I must add that they were harmless, these practical jokes, and perpetrated always in order to please.

This generous desire to give pleasure, so signally lacking in their two surviving great-nephews, must have been a characteristic of that generation of great-uncles, because Etienne's older brother, Armand, did tricks. Taciturn almost to the degree of pathological melancholy, Armand van de Velde was not one you would instinctively associate with an entertainer's skill. Yet there he was, fingers flashing and coloured scarves burgeoning out of thimbles, for all the world as though he had graduated at Maskelyne's Hall of Mystery. Except that there was no patter. All the more effective for that. Throughout his visits a tray was held in readiness, and rung for when it was felt we were due for a display. Under a tablecloth to which was pinned the notice 'Strictly Private and Not to be Inspected' were matchboxes with sliding sides, glasses with false bottoms, an ink-well which at the touch of a button sprouted now a japanese fan, now a paper parasol, a jewel-case in the shape of a miniature cabin trunk with barrelled lid and secrets all its own, an egg-cup with a collapsible egg, and of course the slender ebony wand, silver-tipped and charged with magic, which set the whole thing off. For my part I did not much mind these performances, anyway not until they had been repeated several times, but I was aware of the sturdy determination with which they were watched by the grown-ups. 'One must remember he's very old', was the explanation exchanged for mutual support. Now that I must be nearing the age at which my great-uncle then was, and still do not feel the need to do tricks, I marvel at the charity of my forebears.

Great-uncle Armand was married to a wife of flawless lineage and extreme frailty, who was if anything more solemn, sad, and retiring than himself. 'Don't arf make a chirpy pair,' a housemaid commented to me below stairs. Though almost transparent with delicacy and aristocracy, Great-aunt Heloise ruled her husband with a rod of solicitous affection, bullying the life out of him. Thus it was in obedience to her, and to her sensitivity to draughts, that he wore, summer and winter, a skullcap. Silk in summer, wool in winter. This was better than his brother's toupé, giving him an ecclesiastical or rabbinical look which inspired in me a reverence I hope I would have shown in any case but suspect I would not. Unlike another of his brothers, Edouard, Armand was fond of children but was shy of them. Today a psychiatrist would instance his conjuring as a form of compensation. To his contemporaries it was an indulgence like any other, innocent enough in this case to be humoured.

Differing in age by only a year or two, but otherwise offering marked contrast, was Great-uncle Emil. Here I must confess to a doubt: I am not sure that he was any relation. He was not a van de Velde, so if he was properly a great-uncle he must have been a de Seigneux and my grandmother's brother. However whether blood or courtesy gave him title to it, Emil was 'Uncle Emil' to my own uncles and aunts so can justly be included among his peers. I remember him as the embodiment of good nature and good living. Nothing psychotic here, not a sigh or a groan or a shadow of anxiety, guilt or depression. He wore a little white triangle of beard like an art-dealer and his clothes seemed always on the side of tightness, fitting him like the skin on a ripening plum. His head was bald as could be, but he scorned the toupé and the cap. He moved with a certain swagger, shooting his cuffs for emphasis – a habit regarded as vulgar on this side of the Channel but not, apparently, on the other – and of all who came within the family range he was by far the most exhilarating talker. This alone would make one doubt his blood relationship: certainly from the brothers van de Velde he would not have been up against strong competition. In language and matter, his stories were in the classical tradition: Virgilian images, Homeric exploits. He had thrust his way through jungles, fought in wars, attended tribal rites among primitive peoples, witnessed drumhead courtsmartial and subsequent executions. There seemed to be no part of the world to which Great-uncle Emil had not penetrated, no adventure from the beckoning of which he had turned away. Though I could not have too much of this, I yet had my misgivings. 'But when did Great-uncle *do* all these things?' I asked after a particularly gripping account of a hard slog across Alaska in a blizzard. 'He's lived so long,' my aunt Yolande answered vaguely, 'that I suppose anything may have happened.' 'Oh plenty of time for it,' my father added, 'if you've never done a stroke.' I was not entirely convinced. 'But did he *really* do them?' 'Perhaps when people get to that age, dear,' said Yolande, 'they *feel* they've done them, and things which haven't exactly happened, *seem* as though they had.' This time it is not as in the case of the tricks for I am beginning to know the feeling. By way of correction I must remind myself that I am not truly cut out for scooting the length of the Gobi Desert on camelback and living on cactus soaked in oil. Great-uncle Emil did not look as if he was either, but in these things you can never be quite sure.

From the uncertain provenance of Emil we turn to the indisputable documentation of Edouard. He married Baroness Louisa de Zuylen de Nevelt, and was regarded by both families as an oracle. Perhaps the fact that he rarely spoke lent weight to his utterances; the oracular voice was not one which aired opinions lightly, and for whole days at a time no word would come from him. Like his brother Arthur, my grandfather, he was a mild and troubled man. A gentle disposition was belied by an appearance which was forbidding and even fierce. He wore whiskers which stuck out from his cheeks like wire wool, ready, like the fleece of Gideon, to catch what the elements might give. Dew, fog, and frost would settle on these whiskers — for alone among the brothers he was a keen walker, and after an early morning tramp would appear at the breakfast table looking like a dejected Santa Claus — and one's thought would dwell upon what would happen to them if ever they caught alight. Normally of pallid complexion, at meal times he would become very red in the face, so that three times a day it was thought a stroke threatened. Soon after the last course the flush would subside, and everyone felt relieved. Each year I was warned before his arrival not to remark upon Great-uncle Edouard's changes of colour, and was well content to gaze across the table without comment at a phenomenon which recalled the turning of Egypt's waters into blood in punishment of Pharaoh's obstinacy. In other ways Edouard resembled his brothers, possessing the same pale moist eyes which, somewhat smaller than oysters yet larger than winkles, were in his case the more readily associated with shell-fish by reason of the lobster complexion which drew attention to their prominence. All this was long before blood-pressure was invented.

Edouard was the only member of the family who was at all musical. He played the flute. The accomplishment affected people in different ways, some complaining that he was painful to listen to and others claiming to be proud of having a musician in the family and speaking of the pleasure it gave them to hear him. The truth is that nobody cared enough about music to know whether he played well or badly. But for him it was not just a question of tooting away when he happened to feel like it, which was usually when the senior members of the household were lying down after luncheon and hoping to sleep, but of indoctrination. He was a man with a mission. Moreover he not only played but composed. His compositions he had privately printed under the title *Melodies for Wood-wind,* copies of which he would leave in the rooms of whatever house he was staying in. There was an edition which, for the benefit of his continental friends and relatives, who were presumed capable of reading music but incapable of reading English, while identical as regards the score gave the title in French. It was my father who pointed out that this work was in fact funnier in French on account of reading *'the* wood-wind'. Etienne, the one it will be remembered who disliked Germans, considered his elder brother's musical ventures to be funny any way you looked at them, referring to them as 'old Edouard's flutenfartenspiel'. Excerpts from *Melodies for Wood-wind* were printed separately as Christmas cards — a few lines at a go, little exploratory trills and hoots — which prompted my grandmother's comment that 'melodies should be heard and not seen'.

In suggesting earlier in this study that Edouard disliked children I may be arguing from the particular to the general, and as I was about the only child within flute-hearing it is perhaps unfair to judge. If I fidget today on the rare occasions when I have to listen to a concert, I probably did the same then. My mother, fortunately, was as bad as I was about music, and I doubt if either of us would have gone even so far as to echo my grandmother's observation.

TRAVEL, RETREATS, AND GENERAL

A LOURDES PILGRIM

'Now that's the sort of nature,' I said to myself as I watched the little nun, round and rosy, bouncing along the platform at Victoria with her umbrella and fibre suitcase, 'which I ought to have.' Beaming without stop, twinkling away behind her gold-rimmed glasses, sending out from the heart such crackling messages of goodwill, this rubber-ball sister was clearly going to be the life and soul of the pilgrimage.

One doctor had prescribed one thing, another had prescribed something else, and it was decided to send me to Lourdes. Unable to face the effort of meeting people whom I knew, I had chosen a pilgrimage from a north-country diocese to which I was a complete stranger. While not ill enough to be travelling among the sick I was quite ill enough to want to escape notice among the hale. Surveying the crowd on the platform I did not see a face I knew. All the faces looked very hale. Although the hour was early — the printed instructions issued a week before the date of departure insisting that we present our names to the priest-director who would be waiting for us at the ticket barrier at 7.0 a.m. — everyone was in the highest of spirits. I reflected that it must be a particularly close-knit diocese: almost a parish; almost a family. The little nun, compact and flushed and her glasses clouded over with steam from the heat of her cheeks, bounded from one laughing group to another knowing everybody.

Then, ten minutes before we were timed to leave, the Bishop arrived. Slight deferential hush followed by deferential chatter. Together with the other priests who were making the pilgrimage I paid, though anonymously, my respects. The Bishop chaffed his clergy and slapped their backs. The blank stare with which, on kissing his ring, I was greeted I attributed to the fact that I was wearing the habit. After the inauspicious opening, I made for my place in the third-class compartment; but before I had time to consider seriously backing out of the whole thing the priest-director rang a handbell and we all recited aloud a decade of the rosary. Devotions, with ticket-collectors and buffet-attendants in the background, cause me mental discomfort. I told myself not to be a fool.

Off we went, clonking and clattering over the points from one rail to another, rolling past the backs of sooty houses, past drab lines of washing, past spilling dustbins, posters showing tankards and milk-maids and glossy sausages, past a clutter of obsolete cars, motor tyres, rusting iceboxes. A priest came bumping down the corridor, putting his head through the door of each compartment, calling cheerfully all along the line: 'First five verses of Lourdes hymn, page ninety-six in the little blue book . . . first five verses.' I did my best.

The next person to come in was the little nun. I guessed it was she by the welcome she was getting whenever a door slid back. She came in rattling a wooden collection-box on both sides of which was painted, imperatively, in white lettering: GIVE TO GWAMPULA. With a nice fat chuckle for everyone she held the box under all chins except mine. Perhaps the habit I was wearing exempted me. She gave me a knowing look which said 'people like *us* don't have any money'. When she left, having cheerfully fleeced our compart-ment, a sour-faced man who was sitting opposite me in his shirtsleeves, and who looked as if he had spent years being served cold soup and told by the conductor that the bus was too full to admit another passenger, said, 'Right good idea is that, coming round wi' collection while we still got cash in pocket.' Though the observation was made seriously, even a shade bitterly, it provoked laughter among the pilgrims. I had not yet gauged the quality of north-country humour, so perhaps the would-be cynic was an accepted figure of fun north of about Birmingham. 'Nobut daylight robbery were that,' he added, and everybody laughed again.

At Folkestone, hurrying along the platform towards the boat, I almost ran into the Bishop as he was stepping out of his first-class compartment.

'Ah, the Benedictine. I've just looked you up on the list. Funny name. And not wearing our pilgrimage badge I notice. Aren't we good enough for you?'

I found the badge and pinned it on my chest, bang in the middle of the scapula so that everyone could see.

There was something pleasantly old-fashioned about the boat. More accurately there was something pleasant about remembering other boats which really were old-fashioned. The hoots, the whistles, the wet ropes slapping the deck, the smell coming up from the engine-room, the billowing deckchairs and the brasswork on the gangways. Hardly were we under way when the handbell rang out for another hymn, and our voices sounded thin and silly over the sea. Clearly one must not for a minute let go of the little blue book provided by the travel-agent for the pilgrims. Hymns might break out at any time.

'Hubert, you degenerate monk,' said a growling but at that time still young voice behind me, 'do you know any nice French cooks?'

It was Gilbert Harding, hatless and his light suit flapping in the wind. I had not seen him for some years – not since he had come up to me in the sacristy at Belmont Abbey, where he was then teaching and where I was being ordained deacon, and had asked me to lend him five pounds – but from the expression of his face and voice you would have thought we lunched together every day. My dread of meeting people whom I knew evaporated without my realising it. Eagerly I asked him if he was himself a pilgrim with the rest of us, and how was it we had not seen each other on the train?

'Me a pilgrim? Certainly not. I tell you, I'm looking for a cook. Ours packed her things two days ago and left on a bus for Highgate. And as I cannot endure my mother's cooking for long – fortunately nor can she – I thought I would nip over to Dieppe and get one. I'm just out for the day. No luggage.'

'A sort of one-man press gang. Do you expect to find one?'

'No idea. But I've come stuffed with bribes. Who's this rum-looking nun? She seems to know you.'

Holding her collecting-box in front of her like a snow plough, Sister Dorothy was heading towards us through pilgrims and passengers, hale and sick. There were little beads of sweat on her very fair moustache, and her smile was the sweetest thing this side of Peter Pan. A little flick of the wrist, and Gilbert Harding was being asked to give money to the missions.

'No good here, I'm afraid, Sister. I've got nothing but Turkish currency. But try the monk; he's rolling.'

'I wouldn't embarrass him,' said the nun, with thoughtfulness written all over her. 'Besides I never like begging from people I know. Father has forgotten me; he meets so many nuns in the work he does. But Father gave us such a lovely retreat at Littlehampton that *I* haven't forgotten *him*.' Both of us were included in the warm knowing smile and she was off with her box and her quest.

'Isn't she an old dear,' I said, 'I do so admire that kind of zest and piety.'

'Pretty quick off the mark if that's what you mean. We've hardly weighed anchor, and she's touching everybody from the Captain downwards. That little sister is the kind of woman who is a menace in every society, Greek or Roman, Christian or Moslem. There are some women who must be *getting* things the whole time.'

'But, Gilbert, she's not getting them for herself. And you can see from her face that she's bubbling over with kindness. That smile. She's friendliness personified.'

'I've noticed this before in you, Hubert. You don't make balanced judgments; you form instant impressions. It is something you should correct. I say — ' as we watched someone drop a pound note into the box — 'Gwampula isn't doing too badly.'

'Say what you like, she's going to be a lot jollier than some of my fellow pilgrims.'

'Is she? Remember what Bismark said of Napoleon III: "That man is a sphinx without a secret". Well I think your dear little nun is a smile without a Giaconda. And incidentally did Father give that retreat at Littlehampton?'

'Never been near the place.'

There is this about a pilgrimage to Lourdes that until you are actually there, and sometimes until you have got half-way through the eight days, the temptation to quit is strong. Leaning on the broad rail and looking at the patterns of foam forming on the water, I felt the attraction of spending a day in Dieppe looking for cooks. And then back to England the same night without having opposite me in the train the sour man who sat in his shirtsleeves pulling life to bits. This is what Gilbert Harding advised, and he could be persuasive.

'While you're thinking it over I'll go below. You'll find me in the saloon: it's getting on for my drinking time.'

Primly I told him I thought it would not do for me to join him at the bar. Particularly as a pilgrim. And in a monastic habit. But perhaps even in any case. No, it would not do.

'Absolute rubbish,' he said, his words crunching a gravel drive, 'you chaps with your puritanical notions are a drag on the Church. If Chaucer met you on a pilgrimage he'd cut you dead.'

'But his was the age of faith. Monks and friars could drink regardless and nuns could tuck away in public. Not now any more.'

'Self-consciousness coming in as the faith goes out? The Garden of Eden all over again. Perhaps you're right. Anyway you know where I am if you change your mind. And when you get back from your dreary pilgrimage you must come to dinner and see how the new French cook is getting on.'

It was ten years before I saw Gilbert Harding again, but as I was getting off the boat Sister Dorothy told me she had had a nice little talk with my friend while she was collecting for Gwampula in the saloon, and that he had been most generous.

Grace triumphed and I struggled on. Past farms and fields and cardboard chateaux, past striped awnings, peeling posters showing leopards bursting through paper hoops, matchbox stations, hay-carts, ox-wagons, water-tanks, motor bicycles, slouching soldiers, policemen ready at any minute to burst into action. Slowing down as we thud over the sleepers into Paris, slipping to another rail, hissing and spitting as we fall behind in the race with another train which passes us roaring in its superiority. Then out of Paris again at the other side, and southwards into the night. Fitful sleep in the rattle and rush. The unexplained necessity of speed if it is only to be followed by interminable waits. The mystery of silence in the heart of noise. Dark stations, vaulted in steel, ringing to the sound of high heels on the concrete. Breathless engines, panting out jets of noisy white steam, hauling drugged bodies farther and farther from where they belong. That elderly woman with the teeth and the spotted blouse is eating a sandwich. Imagine, at one in the morning. So it is not a mouse in the waste-paper basket after all, but just a hungry housewife from somewhere north of Birmingham fumbling with tissue paper.

At four-thirty in the morning I opened a yellow eye to see Sister Dorothy pecking like a kindly plover at the glass of the compartment.

What could I do for her I asked? The train was drawn up at a station the name of which I could not see. In the corridor stood men and women from England conscientiously wondering whether they might or might not use the lavatory while the train remained stationary.

'An added jewel for your crown, Father. I ask you to come with me to the buffet on the platform to get a cup of tea for poor Father Flanagan and his asthma. Charity calls, Father.'

'Tea is bad for asthma,' I said, and shut my yellow eye.

'Coffee then. I would go alone but I do not speak French. Quick, dear Father, because the train may not be stopping here for long.'

'Coffee is even worse for asthma. Stick to tea. All you have to do if you can't speak French is to hold the forefinger of one hand upright and then place the other forefinger horizontally on top of it. It's the esperanto sign for tea. All right, all right, Sister, you win. Just let me get on my boots.' (Boots to me are anything in leather that covers the feet.) 'But it has occurred to you of course that you won't be able to get either tea or coffee at this hour.'

'The buffet is open, Father, as I saw when the train was slowing down.'

'You think of everything.'

'It's my job.'

'Your job?'

'To think of everybody's needs.'

'Of course.'

She was right about the place being open. We pushed through the door and were met with a blast of Camembert, French cigarette smoke, coffee grounds, garlic, hot railwaymen. It was evidently the hour at which men working on the line had their breakfast. A faded woman behind the counter, who was wearing a stole of brown rabbit over her official blue calico costume, explained patiently that she could not serve passengers. Believing that the train behind us might start at any moment I was relieved at hearing this, and translated the information into English.

'Tell her about Father Flanagan's asthma.' Without going into it very deeply I must have made out a case because in no time I was holding a bowl of strong, hot, patriotically French coffee. Back on the platform I could see officials running and waving their arms at us.

They appeared to be angry, shouting 'Mais . . . avec les pélérins c'est toujours comme ca . . . en voiture, en voiture . . . je vous prie, mon père, ma soeur . . . *mais* . . . qu'est-ce qu'ils font?' Between puffs of fierce white smoke which issued at regular intervals all along the train I saw heads leaning out of windows. The pilgrims did not look so chummy as when I had seen them on the platform at Victoria not twenty-four hours ago. Was it perhaps another pilgrimage altogether? By now, with the coffee slopping over the bowl and scalding me, I was running along the side of the moving train. Moreover I was alone, for Sister Dorothy, not burdened as I was, had made a better pace and had popped in at a carriage door held open by friendly hands. Had it not been for the strong arm of the Bishop, who had been summoned from his *wagon lit* to meet the crisis, I would have been left behind. Standing in the corridor of a first-class carriage, and wearing a dark red silk dressing-gown over his pyjamas, the Bishop admitted me to his thoughts.

'I hope you realise that while you were in that restaurant guzzling your breakfast, this whole pilgrimage has been held up? Couldn't wait, I suppose, to eat at a reasonable hour in the dining-car with everyone else? I would have thought that living in a monastery would make people less independent and more thoughtful. While travelling with this pilgrimage, kindly stay on the train in future.'

When I got back to my own lower-class carriage I found Sister Dorothy with a sweet smile on her face waiting for me. The coffee, though there was less of it than there had been, was still hot so she took it from me and bumped her way along the corridor towards Father Flanagan's asthma. I thought of Gilbert Harding as I had last seen him, with his hair blowing about and his tie swept over his shoulder as he stepped across the raised threshold into a world which had little to do with bishops and nuns and Father Flanagan's asthma. At this moment he was still in bed, and would be for another three hours.

It took a full twenty-four hours for Lourdes to win me over. From then on I was its slave. To give a day-to-day account of that pilgrimage would be tedious, so I shall mention only those incidents which relate to what has been said. Since for me there is no place in the world with such a variety or such an intensity of association, the ensuing narrative will have to be subject to the strictest discipline.

The coffee incident behind us, the pilgrimage was pretty straightforward stuff. What remained of the train journey was not unpleasant. With the increasing heat the coatless man became collarless as well, sitting sour with his wrists supported in the slack of his braces and every now and then producing comments, flat and grey like the little zinc labels which come out of slot-machines, on the *mores* of foreigners. The frail elderly woman with the teeth ate almost without stop from Paris to the foothills of the Pyrenees, everything she saw out of the window reminding her of familiar landmarks at home where she obviously longed to be. The farther south we rattled the more circuses there appeared to be (posters showing elephants with trunks raised cheerfully over their heads and their feet pressed together on an inverted flowerpot with stars on it, seals with particoloured balloons on their noses, clowns and ringmasters and prancing white horses with girls in tights balancing upright on their backs), the more painted advertisements for the ubiquitous Byrrh, the more frequently repeated threesomes of men in straw hats painting something on each other's backs, the more skittish middle-aged bounders toasting invisible beauties and wearing the improbable combination of dress clothes and white spats (can this ever have been the fashion, even in France?), until at last, after an unforgettable glimpse of Lourdes from across the river, we sighed to a succession of jerks which must have been torture to the sick on the train, and there we were.

The pilgrims were split up into a number of hotels according to either wealth or previous experience. At the Hotel Cachot, curiously but not inappropriately named, there were only two besides myself who wore the enamel badge of the north. Since the hotel was situated near the Cachot itself, where the Soubirous family had lived for a time, it meant a longish walk to the basilicas and the Grotto. I did not mind this: it meant that I was farther away from the better-class hotels, that I was nearer to the station in case I decided to bolt, and that Sister Dorothy would think twice about coming up the steep hill to look for me if Father Flanagan's asthma should happen to take a turn for the worse.

What I did mind however was the smell. It is the only house I have ever been in which included the simultaneous smells of mouse and cat. I had always believed that in such a conflict the mouse smell would inevitably give place to the smell of cat. But there were other smells as well, in strong competition. There were noises too which for ever will be associated in my mind with the Hotel Cachot: the piano played late at night by the daughter of the house, the cries of abuse directed by the same young woman at friends living across the street, the shrill laughter belonging to a third party which greeted these sallies, the bad-tempered barking of a dog with a taste for the seamy side of life.

My fellow countrymen in the hotel, my fellow pilgrims, were puzzled by what they found abroad but not in the least dismayed. Husband and wife, they were determined to share the little adventure together. They seemed anxious too to share it with me. Cut off as we three were from the main stream of the pilgrimage, we were much thrown together. To me my French had always seemed abominable but to them it was the word which unlocked doors. They did not like the 'funny tang' of the bread, so I explained to them, as though I was delivering a broadcast in a schools programme on the habits of North Borneo aborigines, that French bread was never designed to be eaten in a civilised manner with butter and marmalade and washed down with Lipton's tea but was meant to be dipped in coffee or red wine and slopped into the mouth all anyhow. 'You live and learn, Father, that's what I always say. No mistaking it, Father, it takes all sorts.'

The priest-director of our pilgrimage was a man of resource, securing for our group the privilege of Midnight Mass in the basilica of the Rosaire. Since I was already converted by this time, challenged by none in the fervour of my responses to the invocations outside the baths, I put myself down for the Mass which was to be said at the altar of the Ascension. Sister Dorothy of course was there for it, and in order to escape her afterwards I made my thanksgiving as far away as possible – at the Grotto – and then took the half-hour's walk back to the hotel. It was two in the morning when, getting into bed and wanting to prolong my state of holy euphoria with a chapter from the life of Bernadette, I found I had left my glasses at the Rosaire. Unable to read and unwilling to risk delaying it until daylight, I dressed and went down the hill to the Rosaire. The Rosaire was locked, so I walked back again towards the hotel. A light rain was falling, an enormous watch suspended outside a clocksmith's told me that the time was ten to three, and my holy euphoria had entirely evaporated.

After two hours in bed I made the journey to the Rosaire once more, hoping to find the glasses where I knew I had left them, at the *lavabo* by the side of the altar, but they had gone. I tried two sacristans, one sickly but willing and the other snarling and disillusioned, and during the course of the morning visited various lost-property offices, ecclesiastical and civil. Since I could not read without glasses and had recited none of that day's office, I went to an optician's and bought a new pair. It proved a lengthy business because I had no prescription with me, and after a perfunctory testing they gave me a frame which did not fit and two lenses which coordinated imperfectly. I found I could read only by shutting one eye.

Holy euphoria restored, I spent a happy afternoon at the Grotto catching up on the breviary. Before I had anything like finished my devotions a now familiar voice whispered, 'I don't want to interrupt you, Father,' so I took my hand down from the eye I was not using and said, 'In that case, Sister Dorothy, I shall be ready in forty minutes.' Happy still, but holy euphoria had gone again.

'The Bureau closes at six each evening, so I am afraid I must ask you to hurry.'

'Ah, then you do want to interrupt me,' I said, learning now to be just a little bit more like a bishop. 'What Bureau?'

'I can't pronounce the name in French, but it's the office from which they arrange to send Lourdes water by post. It's the building next to where all the confessions are heard, across the road from the topmost basilica. If we go now we can still catch them. I know a short cut.'

'I bet you do.' I put away the breviary and dodged my way after her as she snipped through the silent crowd which watched in front of the Grotto. We reached our goal in plenty of time, and in my atrocious French I managed the complicated negotiations which

41

involved signatures, forwarding addresses, currency exchange. I took my hand down from the more faulty of the two lenses, and made ready to part from Sister Dorothy. We had done our good deed.

'That reminds me. Your glasses. You left them in the chapel after Midnight Mass. Here they are.'

Although the pilgrimage exercises kept us all pretty busy, there were times in the day when one might draw secular breath. It was during these periods of recreation that I found myself getting caught up in a Belgian pilgrimage which had come to Lourdes a day later than our own. Two or three of the Belgians were known to me already — one indeed was a distant relative, and this is not so surprising since everyone in Belgium claims kinship with everyone else and I am myself half Belgian — and others I came to know instantly. The Belgian pilgrimage swarmed all over Lourdes but the particular party to which I refer were staying at the Moderne. Since the bishop who was leading our English pilgrimage was staying at the Moderne, and since a number of other bishops seemed to be staying there too, I judged it to be more in accordance with my station to meet my new friends in humbler settings. They would not have liked the Hotel Cachot, where all the guests ate at a single table, and strips of fly-paper hung down from the lampshade over the communal dishes, so when we had done with wheeling and bathing and feeding and praying with the sick we would meet at a cafe' and recount the events of our day.

In Belgium the code governing introductions is (or used to be thirty years ago) inclined to be rigid. But at Lourdes introductions come easily, as they must when you are meeting people elbow-to-elbow in hospital wards, in processions, lining up for the baths, carrying stretchers and pulling wheeled chairs, so it was no surprise to find a group of American boys and girls attaching themselves to our number. The Americans too were staying at the Moderne.

In each pilgrimage one day is set aside as an off-duty occasion for going on a trip. There are caves to explore, churches to visit, mountain peaks to scale, waterfalls to photograph, and even the distant expensive sea to swim in at places like Biarritz and St Jean de Luz. Luxury buses can carry you far from the incense and candles, from the

42

banners and vestments and invocations. It is astonishing how quickly you can shake off the straps of the *brancardier*. It is also gratifying to find how glad you are to be back in it all at the end of the day. During the torchlight procession you wonder why you were such a fool as to waste eight or nine hours. These things I learned on another occasion, years later.

Be this as it may, I was by now so much part of the young Belgian-American gang that it was taken for granted I would spend the day off with them. There were enough of us to charter a small bus of our own, and we spent some agreeable hours at our favourite streetside cafe' studying maps and contradicting one another. Finally it was arranged that the bus should come to the Moderne at nine next morning, that I should meet them there, and that we should be back in time for the evening meal and the torchlight procession.

As I was walking up the hill after this open-air session, back to my Cachot with its vinegar on the table even at breakfast, I sensed impending disaster. More accurately I heard Sister Dorothy's step behind me and *then* smelled trouble.

'Your hotel is not on the telephone so I could not get you before,' cooed Sister Dorothy, 'but tomorrow is our *dies non*, you know, the day we have no pilgrimage obligations.' Had she already, with her grape-vine working all out, learned of the Belgian-American venture and was now proposing to tag on? No, it was not that, but from my point of view it was every bit as bad. She wanted to spend tomorrow morning in consultation with me about her spiritual state.

'Sister, I have already arranged to go out with some friends.'

'I know, Father, and I would not want to disappoint them. I never put people out if I can possibly help it. But your engagement for tomorrow is after all only *social* is it not? It is not a matter of winning souls. My need, Father, is a spiritual one. How would you feel afterwards, Father, if you knew you had turned down an offer of grace?'

It was blackmail of course, but there was no way out. I asked her to give me an hour to think about it and I would let her know. I would telephone to her hotel from a call-box. Where was she staying?

'The Moderne, Father. Reverend Mother likes us to stay there because it is nearer to the churches and the Grotto.'

43

'Of course.'

'And your nice young friends are staying there too, so if you come back now with me you can explain and then let me know the best time for you to see me tomorrow.'

I felt there was more vinegar in me at that moment than in the dining-room at the Hotel Cachot. For sourness I could have met on equal terms with the cynical pilgrim of the railway carriage (and who now, by the way, was to be seen at every pilgrimage duty with the badge pinned gallantly to his braces, so perhaps the Bishop had been at him too) and outclassed him in a straight fight.

'I suppose you must,' said one of the Belgians, 'especially as she's such a dear little soul.'

What was Gilbert Harding whispering in my ear? In that voice like a slow wave breaking on the shingle I heard him say 'dear little soul, my foot'.

So it was settled that Sister Dorothy would find me waiting for her at eleven next morning in the domestic chapel of the Sept Douleurs. It would be quiet in there, she told me, and it would give us a clear hour before she had to resume her good works — dishing out lunches to the sick at the Sept Douleurs.

I found the chapel without difficulty. It was upstairs, and, as she had said, quiet. So quiet that I was able to do the Stations of the Cross, read my office, and meditate without once being interrupted. The lonely vigil was brought to a close only when one of the community explained apologetically that she had to lock up for the luncheon hour.

I asked at the desk, but all the Moderne could tell me was that the *très charmante* little English sister had left the hotel early in the morning with some guests who planned to take her for a drive to the coast. They did not know if Sister would be back for the evening meal. *Bien sur* my own friends, the Belgians and Americans, had left punctually at nine. His Excellency was even now having luncheon, and would I care perhaps to join him at his coffee?

'It was a chance in a lifetime,' Sister Dorothy told me next morning, 'and I knew you wouldn't mind. When these dear people invited me I said to myself, "Sister, you may be able to do them good: they are lonely and rich and getting on in years: go with them in their car, even if it means visiting worldly towns and keeping Father waiting: see what you can do." And it was wonderful how generous people were in those big smart places. Gwampula will be proud of poor old Sister Dorothy.'

'I'm sure.'

Most would agree that leaving Lourdes is a painful experience. If the hand on the spiritual barometer had wobbled a bit at times, now that the eight days were over it stood as steady as the spire on the basilica. If I had looked forward to one kind of miracle to result from my pilgrimage I was forced to acknowledge another. For the first time in ages I could view all mankind without malice, and if this does not in my case posit a miracle I would like to know what does.

Nor was I the only one to receive favours. What favours the sick received is not for me to say. Looking along the departure platform on the last morning at my fellow pilgrims it was the hale whom I was then considering. To the original chumminess from which I had shrunk at Victoria Station — was it only eight days ago? — something was now added.

The Bishop for instance. Perhaps Lourdes had lowered his blood-pressure or done something to his ulcers, but there he was in the warm sun gently teasing me about being a monk who kept trains waiting while finishing his breakfast.

Over there, leaning against the door of his compartment, was the sour man in his shirtsleeves studying the scene with evident enjoyment. Looped in his braces were thumbs to which experience of life may have given a downward direction, but the rest of him pointed to the sky.

My fellow lodgers of the Hotel Cachot were glowing. The lady who had nibbled across the length of France and had seen Runcorn in the landscape which had inspired Ronsard, was mumbling the rosary through her crumbs.

Approaching with her collection-box at the ready — and playfully veiled as though it were a top hat in a conjuring act — was Sister Dorothy.

'Come over here, Sister,' said the Bishop, 'I want you to meet this Benedictine.'

'Oh, we've met already, m'lord. He gave our community retreat some years ago.'

'Did he? He doesn't look old enough. I must get Dom Hubert to give our diocesan retreat.'

'Dom Hubert?' said Sister Dorothy, her face falling steeply. It was the first time I had seen her at a loss. 'But I thought he was Dom Bede Winslow from Ramsgate.'

Since I had so far escaped extortion under false pretences, I was now fair game. Whisking away the cloth, she waggled the collection-box under my chin. Fumbling in my pockets for money I felt something else. I dropped the pair of cockeyed glasses into the box.

'Quits,' she said.

'Quits,' I said.

WE HAD IT COMING TO US, ALLELUIA

'When you've been on one pilgrimage,' a veteran shrine-crawler once told me, 'you've been on the lot.' Nothing could be further from my own experience. Nevertheless it is all too easy to become pilgrimage-prone, and to use the opportunity as an excuse for a little change. For me the excuse came when an uncle of mine wrote to me from Brussels where he was living, or more correctly where he was dying, and suggested that I should come over from my monastery in England to see him. He further suggested that I might make a pilgrimage to the body of my patron St Hubert in the town of that name, which is situated in the heart of the Ardennes. Since the circumstances of this second holy undertaking contrasted sharply with those of the earlier one to Lourdes there will be no danger of repetition. A little pilgrimaging goes a long way, but it is not true to say that in going to Fatima and Walsingham you are only going to Lourdes over again.

Supplied with a map of Belgium, and a blessing upon the project from my superior, I set out from the monastery in a blur of sanctimonious satisfaction. This time it was to be by way of Dover and Ostend, but this time too, as in the case of the year before, I was hailed on the boat by someone I knew. Patrick Robertson, then a lieutenant in the Brigade of Guards, the Grenadiers, (today a colonel), was off on a week's leave. In the confusion of embarkation at Dover, boarding by a more humble gangway than that which took him to his first-class deck, I had observed in the distance the bowler-hat, dark suit, hard collar, rolled-up umbrella, and white pigskin luggage, but had not related these symbols to anyone I knew. So when, as the ship drew away from the quay and footsteps clattered cheerfully down the companion, I heard myself addressed with the formula of the day, 'Hallo, hallo, hallo, what are you doing here?' (the present equivalent is 'How nice to see you') I was taken a little by surprise.

I told of my twofold mission. His mission was more singleminded: he planned to lie in the sun on the beach at Ostend, gamble in the

47

evenings, and go back to Windsor when his leave expired. He seemed puzzled that I should want to leave Brussels so soon – I proposed to leave the day after next – for the forests of the Ardennes. Particularly he seemed puzzled that I should want to do the eighty miles on foot.

'I thought if people made pilgrimages they made them to Lourdes.'

'I went there last year.'

'And it didn't work?'

'It worked all right. But as the only priest in my carriage I had to lead the recitation of the rosary. I never knew the prayer at the end. It was very mortifying.'

'It must have been. Could you not have used a book?'

'It would have looked odd. In this private pilgrimage to St Hubert's shrine that sort of thing won't come up. Why don't you join me? It would do your soul more good than a week in an hotel at Ostend.'

'Thanks. I will.'

Patrick took off his bowler-hat and substituted a tweed cap. The cap, he told me, had been meant only for the channel crossing but would now come in useful for the pilgrimage. In his suitcase there was a straw boater, much more dashing, which had been intended for Ostend: it would not do at all for the pilgrimage. In addition to the pigskin suitcase there was a pigskin hat-box, shaped like an eye-bath, for the bowler.

'Don't throw any of that overboard,' I said; 'you can leave what you don't want at my uncle's and pick it up on the way back. We can spend tonight and tomorrow night with him in Brussels, do our shopping for the necessary equipment tomorrow, and leave at dawn next morning. Averaging fifteen miles a day, and making the return journey by train, we are in Brussels again tomorrow week. We can do it easily.'

'No good. My leave ends today week. On parade next morning.'

'In that case we average twenty miles a day. How fit are you?'

'Fit as a flea. I had no idea you were so efficient.'

I had kept it from him for years.

My uncle and aunt lived in a large over-furnished, over-staffed, and blissfully over-heated house in the Avenue Louise. I had sent a telegram from Bruges, where we stopped for ten minutes, announcing the time of the train's arrival and saying I would be bringing a friend. In order to strengthen Patrick's idea of my efficiency I sent another from Ghent, saying the same thing.

'Why a second one?' Patrick asked.

'The first was to the address. This one is to the telephone number. We want to make sure of being met.'

We were not met, and both telegrams arrived by post next morning.

Our host and hostess were delighted with Patrick. Whenever there was a pause in the conversation one or other of them would say, 'But of course you will never do it in the time.'

We did our shopping independently, both of us knowing that it is easier for two men to spend a week together on the road than half an hour together in a shop. Comparing our purchases when we got home, we agreed on the wisdom of our respective selection. Patrick had bought nailed boots to replace his gentlemanly shoes from St James's, thick socks, a compass and an English-French dictionary. The compass, I suspected, was his way of sending a second telegram. Items on my list were concerned exclusively with securing warmth. My aunt bought me a lined and hooded black rubber cape which reached below the waist, weighed a ton, and made me look like a French policeman. My uncle gave to each of us a rucksack with so rich a complement of pockets that we went out shopping a second time so as to have something to put into them. We bought bars of chocolate, paper handkerchiefs, sticking plaster and medicated gauze.

At five next morning I said Mass at a convent chapel which was dedicated to St Hubert — my uncle had arranged it with the nuns who were enchanted and not dismayed at having to open their door at half past four — and Patrick served. The objects of piety with which we were presented as we set off at six further filled out the pouches on our rucksacks.

'There are trams,' said Patrick, 'which take workmen to the outskirts where the factories are. They run about now.'

'I know,' I said.

'Perhaps you are right. From door to door and no cheating.'

Patrick's studded boots rang on the pavements and must have been very uncomfortable. While we were still in the town his dark pin-stripe suit looked apt enough: in spite of the rucksack, tweed cap, and riding Burberry which completed the ensemble. He had decided to take his hat-box with him after all — the bowler affording better protection in the event of a hailstorm — so, what with his rolled-up umbrella, his accoutrements were more considerable than mine. I was glad to see he had abandoned the hard collar in favour of a flannel shirt, which, even with the Brigade of Guards tie, was more in tune with the Ardennes. My own costume was designedly nearer to that of the medieval pilgrim — I was dressed in the religious habit and carried a stout stick — though alien associations intruded. My wide-brimmed black hat with the depressed crown suggested the bad cowboy of a Western, and there was also the gendarme cape. I had scorned my aunt's offer of an umbrella.

Nor, that day, did we need umbrellas. As the sun rose high in the sky it became clear that there would never again be a hailstorm in Belgium.

What struck us was the contrast between the country we were walking in and the capital we had left behind. Streets in Brussels go up and down as at San Francisco: Belgium's roads are, mercifully for the pilgrim, flat. Though level and straight, many of them are cobbled. Where possible we moved over unpaved ground, and if this added somewhat to the mileage it created the illusion that we were travelling more comfortably. We did well on the first day, coming only a little short of Waterloo which Patrick, as a soldier, wanted to inspect.

You would not expect Waterloo in August to be innocent of trippers, and it was not. The village where we decided to spend the night was aglow with tourists, all of whom seemed to have come on bicycles. The *vélo* is popular in Belgium anyway, but we had hit a cyclists' convention at which every bicycling club in the country must have been represented. We were surrounded by shining wheels, silver tubes, turned-down handle-bars, acetylene lamps which threw out the proportions of everything and looked like tumours, little fluttering nervous pennons of coloured silk printed with a name or a symbol, tightly rolled yellow cylinders of waterproof strapped to the back of the saddle. If the machines all looked alike, so did the young men who rode them. Fair hair bleached by the sun and worn long in front, sun-glasses or even goggles, coloured skull-caps showing the badges of their clubs, black corduroy shorts turned up over bulging muscles, white singlets (more badges), brown arms and legs covered by pale fur, white ankle-socks, strangely feminine low-heeled shoes of dappled leather with laces tipped with cloth acorns. In the middle of what might have been the *Tour de France* taking an evening off, we doubted if we would be able to find rooms for the night.

We tried the curé and were rewarded. At each of the places where we hoped to spend the night it was necessary to make arrangements for Mass the next morning, and not once did a curé fail us. On this first occasion, after being turned away because of the *vélo* invasion we were directed by the priest to the schoolmaster's house.

'Monsieur Tiffard will be busy,' the priest told us; 'he is not important. It is Madame with whom you must deal. She will prove important. Monsieur is a so-so kind of man. Of no importance.'

How Madame did it, with Brabant's swift-peddling youth on her hands, I cannot imagine. Patrick and I were asked to share a room but since we had resigned ourselves to sharing a hayloft we were not dismayed. We were even given an excellent supper. Monsieur Tiffard was not, certainly, important. I had always understood that village schoolmasters spent their evenings either correcting exercise-books or catching up on their reading. Monsieur Tiffard spent his knitting.

The cyclists talked all night, their snatches of conversation coming to us through the fog of sleep from different parts of the house. Every now and then someone would bang on a wall and for a bit there would be quiet and we would hear an owl from somewhere on the field of Waterloo.

Cyclists and pilgrims are early risers. I could hear tyres being pumped before I had finished shaving. Calling him at the time we had fixed, I asked Patrick how he was feeling after yesterday.

'In top gear,' he said, and went to sleep again.

That was the day it got really hot. My black rubber cape had me streaming inside its smooth glossy shell.

'I thought you liked the heat,' said Patrick.

'I do. How are your feet in those boots?'

'Just right.'

From Waterloo, which Patrick found disappointing, we walked to

Ramillies. The wars were getting their whack out of us. We arrived as the sacristan was closing the church, but the sight of us so stimulated him that he thrust looking-glasses into our hands and prepared himself to show us every relic, every picture, every chalice and vestment.

'What are we supposed to do with these?' Patrick asked me as we sat, unable to take another step, with the looking-glasses on our laps,

'I think they must be for the paintings on the ceiling.'

'Don't tell me he's going to drag us up there.'

The kindly sacristan's intentions were wasted. We were taking root in the benches.

The hotel which the curé recommended did not appeal to us, and as we were too tired to look for another we decided to sleep under the stars. At nine it was still the kind of heat I like, and at ten it was merely a question of dealing with the midges and mosquitoes.

'I'd rather have midges than those *vélo* chaps,' said Patrick.

Somewhere between Ramillies and Namur we came to the conclusion that if we were to get to St Hubert in time we would have to cast off ballast. We looked at our packs, which were bulging, but were reluctant to make sacrifices. Patrick gave his tweed cap to a man who was working at a telegraph pole. The man looked pleased so I gave him two woollen shirts and some woollen stockings. In Namur Patrick bought a dazzling panama and a pair of sunglasses, and felt better. I bought two cotton shirts, but this was no extravagance because my back was coming out in a rash and what I could see of it looked like a raw steak. I did not pine for wool.

Crossing the Meuse at Namur and seeing the great fortress on the hill so set our historical pulses throbbing that we bought a guidebook. It weighed at least as much as a woollen shirt.

'Well, I'm not going to get rid of my Locke bowler or my Briggs umbrella if that's what you mean.'

Following a tributary of the Meuse called the Lesse we headed due south (according to the compass which Patrick was at pains every few hours to consult) and made for the gay-sounding town of Dinant. We reached an inn somewhat short of Dinant at sunset and could go no farther. Again it was the lady of the house and not the husband who took charge. She told us she had a special dish which she was in the habit of serving to 'les Alpinistes'. We said we were much interested. It turned out to be a massive soup, brought to the table in a dainty flowered tureen which made one think of a shepherdess playing up to a centaur. The soup appeared to contain everything that grows except a Christmas tree. I chose, at the risk of offending madame, to stick to sour bread and cheese. Even sitting well back from the tureen I could feel the pepper in it snapping at me. It was an angry, foot-stamping, soup.

'I like soup and you don't,' said Patrick, stirring its questionable depths, 'it's as simple as that.'

That night I dreamed that the sacristan at Ramillies was pouring methylated spirits over my back and touching it off with a taper.

Patrick did not say much next day, but I did not put this down to the soup. I thought he might be regretting his deckchair at Ostend, and the roulette table. Since I could not carry the rucksack against my shoulder-blades I had to trail it at my side, shifting it at intervals from one hand to another. I was glad I had decided against bringing my typewriter.

At Dinant, which did not live up to its name, we struck off south-east and pushed through some densely forested country. We did our twenty miles, but only just.

It rained during the night and for most of the day following. This made the going easier — if only because Patrick was able to pit his bowler against the downpour and I my policeman's cape.

Surprisingly, except that nothing should surprise one on the road, we ran into a jolly crowd of men, women, and children wearing masks and funny hats and blowing paper hooters. Everyone was jumping about and laughing. The whole thing was on the move, and, settled awkwardly in a haycart, was a brass band blowing its head off. On other carts were jugs and barrels and crates of food. By the time we drew level on the long road through the woods, the revellers had decided to accept us among them. We were offered beer, toffee-apples, sweet biscuits, doughnuts, and something black and sticky which was cut up into slabs and was awash in great metal trays. It is a strange thing to be offered food by people whose faces you cannot see, whose language you cannot understand, and whose presence you cannot account for. The English-French dictionary was no use here. Walloon? Flemish? Dutch? It did not matter. The rain did not matter. Nothing mattered. They were eating oranges out of wet tambourines from which hung paper streamers.

We pressed on. Patrick was looking pale green and limping.

'Those boots?' I asked.

'A bit. They will be all right when they're broken in.'

'You don't look up to much.'

'I never look my best during a cloudburst. How are the heat-bumps?'

'Still itching. That's why I'm walking like this.' (The blisters had spread to my sides so I was keeping my arms away from the body.)

'Perhaps they're not heat-bumps but ants. That night we slept on the ground.'

The next stage remains uncertain in my memory. There were periods of scorching sun and heavy showers. The villages got farther apart as we got deeper into the Ardennes. Our immediate objective was Rochefort where I knew there was a Trappist monastery which would put us up before we made our final assault on the town of St Hubert. The map showed the Abbey of St Remi as only about eleven miles from St Hubert.

'I wish you would get into the way of calculating by kilometers,' said Patrick. He added, 'I think we're lost.'

Coming towards us, wheeling a bicycle, was a short white-faced young man who looked peculiar. It was the first human being we had seen for hours.

'Here's just the chap,' I told Patrick, 'try him out on your kilometers.'

Patrick's kilometers left the young man unmoved. He shrugged his shoulders and made as if to pass on. I knew he would be the last person whom we were likely to meet for some time. So I stood in his way, and when he pointed his bicycle to one side or the other I jumped. Patrick sat down on the road and undid his boots.

'St Remi . . . *moines* . . . *abbaye*,' I shouted at him, thinking he might be deaf. He was not deaf; it was only that he was 'simple', and

54

that neither of us knew the other's language. He did not know even as much French as I did. So I tried pantomime. I pointed to the habit I was wearing. I took off my cowboy hat and put my hood up. It worked.

'Aha!' he cried, his face lighting up, *'Brüder . . . Brüder . . . ehe, Brüder.'*

'Oui, Brüder, whatever language that is. Exactly that, *Brüder.'*

'Three cheers,' said Patrick from the side of the road while smearing Vaseline over his feet.

The young man was kindness itself. He put our packs on his bicycle, one on the saddle and one on the handle-bars, and walked with us for a considerable distance until we saw the abbey spire sticking up from a belt of trees like a magician's hat. Our gratitude was boundless but he would take no money. We gave him some clean socks and a cardigan.

At the monastery we were received by the monks as though we had been in touch with them for years and had at last managed to come. The abbot was away but the prior turned us over to the guestmaster, and the guestmaster, without prompting from us, turned us over to the infirmarian. Patrick was given aspirins, hot brandy and water, and sent to bed. His boots were taken from him to be beaten by hammers overnight, to make further travel softer on the foot. The blisters on my back and sides were pronounced to be neither heat-bumps nor the ravages left by ants.

'It is the harvest-bug,' the infirmarian told me in American-English (he had done his studies in Rome, he told me, at the Order's international college), 'but we have the remedy. Sure. Quite a few of us suffer from the harvest-bug, but our Brother Conrad makes a preparation of his own which cools the irritation. Guess I'll ask our Brother Conrad to come by. Please God he'll fix this bug real good.'

Our Brother Conrad's preparation was applied, and when I got my breath back I had to admit that it brought a measure of relief. It was forbidding to look at, dark brown, and still more forbidding to smell. They put a little jar of it in one of the pockets of my rucksack, and when I asked its ingredients I was told that our Brother Conrad had his secrets. 'He has made a study,' was all I could learn, 'of the fats of the Belgian wild boar.'

'And my friend's feet,' I asked the infirmarian, 'how are they getting on?'

'Not making out too good. He is in a tough spot.'

'Tomorrow after Mass,' I said, 'we march.'

That evening I telephoned from the monastery to a young man I had been at school with, indeed to whom I believe I am distantly related, who lived about twenty miles from St Hubert. This was Jean van der Straten-Waillet. I explained about Patrick and myself not being in fighting trim, and could he put us up for a night at Waillet before we went back to Brussels? He said he would be glad to, so we arranged to meet at St Hubert in the afternoon of the following day. He would drive us to Waillet, where I had stayed once before, and we could rest as long as we liked. The omens were propitious.

The prior offered to have us taken by car to St Hubert but we would have none of it. We said goodbye, setting our faces south-south-east towards St Hubert. (Ten years later, after the war and with great profit to my soul, I paid a second visit to the Trappists of St Remi.) This represented the last lap, a mere twelve miles, of our pilgrimage. We were determined to acquit ourselves with dignity.

Dignity did not come easily. Patrick was wearing gymshoes given to him as a farewell present by the monks. I had thrown away my pilgrim's staff in order to leave one hand free to hold my shirt away from my chest, which was bubbling like boiling fish. Our Brother Conrad's specific had lost its power. At the end of every mile we sat on the ground and rested. Our approach to St Hubert was anything but majestic. A feature of this final stretch was the number of people in cars or on carts who, taking a good look at us, offered to give us lifts. After meeting hardly any traffic on the road the day before we were now almost jostled by it. And everyone in the neighbourhood who moved on wheels however humble seemed charitably bent upon easing our course.

In the early afternoon we reached St Hubert. The great honey-coloured church was a surprise to both of us, its beauty and its setting surely one of the noblest sights in Belgium. Trailing past lemonade sold from trestle tables, objects of piety exhibited in tiers, old ladies in black sitting in the shade of umbrellas, staring and dribbling children, dogs sniffing with the rudeness of their kind, hens bad-tempered in the heat, we dropped our packs in the shelter of the porch and went in.

Nobody knows in exactly what part of the building St Hubert's body lies buried, but this bothered neither of us. From the nave, dark in contrast to the glare outside and as cool as an aquarium, we paid our respects. Worship, petition, thanksgiving. To these was added, speaking for myself, relief. Not relief that it was over: relief that nothing had happened which had turned us back.

Slowly (perforce) we walked round the church but it was a listless tour, perfunctory and from a sense of duty. We were drained of interest, so instead of lingering with a guidebook, the weight of which was no longer a consideration, we came away. Picking up our packs, and pushing through the flies which hung about in clouds, we made towards the open-air cafe' which bordered the *domaine* and at which Jean had arranged to meet us. The sellers of lemonade, which was both on draft and in bottles, were disappointed in us. Still more so were the sellers of rosaries which in all colours and sizes dripped from hooks. But they had been disappointed before now, and had learned to bear with it. Not even the peeling rectangular building on the right which had housed generations of Benedictine monks two centuries earlier was able to evoke from me the appropriate responses. At this stage the only thought in my head was wondering which part of me was skin and which was shirt.

'Counting the extra distance of going out of our way so that you could play soldiers at Waterloo,' I said as we creaked on to the silly tin chairs of the cafe', 'I make it eighty-four miles.'

'Just about. Or in kilometers . . . '

Jean arrived in a long, black, shining American car with his mother and his brother Alec. Baroness van der Straten-Waillet, to celebrate both our meeting again and the successful conclusion of the pilgrimage, ordered champagne.

So it was that when a rather ramshackle car of English make drew up, we presented to the two men who got out of it a picture of pleasing relaxation. It so happened that one of these men I knew, Walter Hobden, a journalist and one-time editor of a literary magazine. The younger man, who was driving, I did not know. Many years my senior, Walter Hobden was at that time, as he explained when the introductions were over, renewing his youth by travelling about with his nephew and collecting material for a book about the Napoleonic wars. Certainly he looked spry enough, for all his sixty years, and fat. Jaunty even, in his bow tie and light summer suit. He was always the genial man of culture, but today was more than ever genial. As though he had suddenly come upon us in the wastes of the Sahara.

I noticed that while he talked, which he did with animation and fluency, he was not letting much escape him. And what did he see? Glasses and two bottles of champagne on the table, the long black car in the background, Patrick's face proclaiming the unwholesome mushroom pallor of the cave dweller, my own face (the only one present which he knew) puffy from sleeplessness and not much healthier than Patrick's. He was talking to the Baroness.

'When I was their age,' he was saying of us with the breezy assurance of one whose own age places him comfortably beyond the challenge and the joust, 'I would have done this trip of mine over the battlefields on foot and thought nothing of it. Your two sons look fit enough, Baroness, and that's because of the kind of life you Belgian families lead out here in the country. But if you ask me, what these two Englishmen need is a bit more fresh air and exercise.'

Back in England once more, Patrick spent the next ten days in bed being treated for food poisoning. I, looked after in my monastery, had shingles.

MOTHER MELANIE

'Reverend Mother has the lumbago,' said a fresh-faced Irish sister as I presented myself this morning at the front-door of the convent, 'and she'll not be up to seeing you.'

'Oh yes she will,' said a voice some way down the narrow hall, 'bring him along, whoever he is.' I was brought along.

On Friday night when I arrived, I was told I would have to teach catechism and scripture at the school, and that I had better find out from Reverend Mother exactly what was wanted — the syllabus, curriculum and so on — before my first appearance in the classroom on Monday morning. So, with a list of questions in my pocket and a sinking feeling in my chest (for if there is one role in the world for which I know myself to be unsuited it is that of school-teacher), I went round to the convent before luncheon. The playground, as it was Sunday, was mercifully deserted, and it was only after I had rung at three doors that I realised I had come to the wrong part of the establishment. From Friday evening till Monday morning, the nuns must be living on the other side of the building. The school is mustard-coloured brick, with what seems an unnecessary amount of ironwork on the outside. It is hideous. The convent is hideous too, but in a different way. It is an older building, grey stone walls and slate roof, and was once a private house. I would put its date about 1830 but it has, in an absent-minded way, been added to at intervals over the years and now looks like a shabbily dressed but very genteel old lady who has given up trying. The school stands apart from the convent, as if to show that there is no competition, but is connected by a temporary cloister made of a fabricated material which I believe is called 'eternite' and roofed with corrugated iron. I can guess what this connecting corridor looks like on the inside and what it contains: linoleum floor, framed holy pictures and a signed photograph of the bishop, pots of ferns. I shall be able to verify this (or contradict it) later in the week if it is to be the way which I shall take from the classroom to the chapel.

At the sound of her superior's voice, the Irish sister spun round and led me to a door over which was painted in Gothic lettering 'Saint Francis Xavier'. As if to forestall a confusion of identity, a card pinned to the door itself read 'Reverend Mother'. The door was half open, so all the sister had to do was to usher me in and then vanish. The impression I had was that she could not get away quickly enough.

'Forgive me for not getting up, Father, but as you have just learned from the health bulletin which Sister Malachy seems to be promulgating I am troubled at the moment by lumbago. She called it, if you noticed, *the* lumbago. Like the plague or the king's evil. Not that it signifies. Well, you must be the temporary priest — or I should say the priest who is to help us temporarily. *Tu es sacerdos in aeternum.* I was expecting, for no reason whatever, someone older. But perhaps it is just as well you are new to the job, and can bring to it the still undimmed illusions of the young. These children to whom you will be breaking the bread of Christian knowledge tomorrow morning are the dearest souls imaginable — I love each one of them with a mother's heart — but you can bet your boots they will put you through it. Now may I have your name? Mine is Melanie des Anges. I won't translate. Address me simply as "Reverend Mother"; the other members of the community you call "Sister".'

She had spoken without a pause; almost it seemed without drawing breath. It was as though she was not speaking to me at all but just quietly amusing herself. I have a feeling she is someone quite remarkable, and must find out more about her. Even in appearance she is striking, and her way of talking — slow, controlled, and on a low note — exactly suits her looks. She has a white complexion, her face covered with lines. But her skin is more like the leaf of a Russian olive than crumpled tissue paper. Her mouth is wide and humorous, slightly mocking yet not quite cynical. Her eyes are grey, shrewd, and unblinking. In fact I wondered if she was trying to stare me out. A nun's age is never easy to guess, but I should say she was about seventy.

I gave her my name and she told me she had known my

great-aunt Wowsie. This surprised me greatly but did not seem to surprise her. I doubt if she is ever surprised by anything: she is as if poised eternally and impervious to shock or novelty or change. When I produced my pencilled list of questions, she smiled. 'But,' I said, 'I have to know how many children are in the classes, what their ages are, and what exams they are supposed to be working for. I don't even know what periods I am expected to teach them as regards scripture, or what chapters as regards the catechism.'

'Oh dear, I hope you are not going to be another of these efficient priests,' she said; 'the children won't like that at all.'

It was my turn to smile: I had never been called efficient before. I pointed out that if the children showed a prejudice against efficiency there were still diocesan examiners to worry about. 'And there's your own headmistress, and even perhaps —' here I brought out what I had been led to believe was invariably a trump card where nuns were concerned — 'the bishop.'

'Don't give a thought,' said this surprising nun, 'to diocesan examiners, headmistresses, or bishops. They're *my* job. All you have to do is to think about the children.' She added, with almost a chuckle, 'I can settle the others with my little finger; it's the children I want settled. And that's where you come in. Good afternoon, Father, and whatever you do avoid getting lumbago.'

After leaving Reverend Mother yesterday I was able, but only after ringing the front-door bell a second time and sheepishly explaining the situation in a whisper to Sister Malachy, to secure an interview with Sister Lioba, the headmistress of the school. She gave me all the information I needed, so after staying up late last night with text-books and typed notes, I appeared at the right door of the right building and at the right time. The children were assembled in the gymnasium for what is called 'announcements', so I did not have to push my way through a staring and giggling crowd. Instead a nun walked me decorously to my appointed rostrum, and I waited there, like the doctor standing in the shadow of the electric chair, till the bell clanged and my pupils poured in.

(I do not propose in these extracts to describe my early struggles in the field of education, so all that has to do with the boys and girls who, between the ages of eleven and fourteen, sat at my feet — if anything as tranquil as sitting can here by applied — each morning for two school periods can be left out. Only where they relate to Mother Melanie will my activities in the yellow-brick part of St Bride's Convent and School be recorded. The account in the diary, broken off at the close of the foregoing paragraph, is resumed at the point where, after my first morning's work, I was handed a note from Reverend Mother asking me to look in before I left.)

Reverend Mother is still confined by lumbago to the room where she works and receives people. When she received me she was playing patience, but she stopped her game when I sat down. I noticed a heap of unopened letters which had not been on her desk yesterday, so evidently she is not one to fuss unduly about business matters in the way that religious superiors tend to do.

'Well,' she said, polishing her glasses with a khaki handkerchief, 'how did it go, the opening manoeuvre?' I said it might have been worse, but that I had not expected as many as sixty in a class. She agreed that the number was far too high, and added, 'But if you teach them properly you will find yourself thinking of them not as a group of sixty but as single individuals who happen to make up a group of sixty. We talk a lot of rubbish about instructing Catholic youth; it's *this youth in front of me now* that I have to instruct. I wouldn't mind betting that Sister Lioba spoke to you yesterday about third-year students and fourth-year students. She has to, poor darling, it's part of her job. But don't make the mistake of thinking about what you are doing in terms of 1930's enrolment, 1931's, this year's and next's. These children are not lists, not stages in a progressive plan, not categories. Don't be dismayed by seeing them as a sixty-sized block. It will look like that at first, but when you begin to distinguish one face from another it will become more like individual tuition applied in sixty different cases. Or rather applied to sixty different individuals: the word "cases" is misleading. What did you talk to them about this morning?'

'I told them about the minor prophets,' I said, 'of whom they had apparently never heard. I must say I am glad you are not tying me down to a set scheme.'

'The secret of it,' she said, though not with the air of one who is giving instruction, 'is never to teach anything which you are not your-self interested in. Of course this limits considerably the teacher's range, but I would rather employ a large staff of people who had only one subject than economise with a small staff who would be ready to teach anything. Since human beings cannot get excited about everything it is not the faintest use their trying to teach everything. You are presumably excited by the minor prophets or you would not have spoken about them to your first class.' I admitted that the minor prophets stirred me.

At this point our conversation was interrupted by a series of explosions: the bursts of sound came only from the radiator but they were so loud that I expected the metal to break and fall apart. From all over the house came similar reports. It was as if an ammunition dump were catching fire bit by bit.

'That would be Gum, the handy-man,' she explained when the first echoes had died down, 'he has probably heard about my lumbago, and is prescribing heat.'

'Gum, Reverend Mother? Surely that can't be his name?'

'It isn't, but he's known by no other. Gum the handy-man. He sounds like something out of a child's book, doesn't he? Well, he's very real indeed I can tell you. A rogue of course, but highly useful to us and devoted to the community. You must meet Gum. Try him out on your minor prophets, and see what he says. But don't let him shock you; he's inclined to be frank.'

'Does he shock you, Reverend Mother?' I asked. She very slowly shook her head and began picking up her cards. The audience was at an end. As I made my way out I could hear the radiators throughout the house gurgling and bubbling. No orchestration could be sweeter to my ears, and I felt grateful to Gum that so early in the autumn he should have turned his attention to the boiler.

I have now finished my first week of teaching at St Bride's. As it happens I was quite wrong in my guess as to what the connecting corridor looks like on the inside. Better than I thought: coconut matting on the floor, no ferns, some Arundel prints well spaced out. Not handsome but simple and decent, even austere. No shades on the hanging electric-light bulbs, no curtains, no flowers. I imagine

63

Reverend Mother must have her hand on this as on all else. Even in the convent itself, graceless as it is from the architectural point of view, there is nothing offensive in the way of furniture or decoration. No velvet table-covers, for example, or embossed brass coal-scuttles, and no china funnel waiting to receive an umbrella. It would be too much to expect nuns to rid themselves of statues which are less than beautiful, but at least here at St Bride's, there is no embarrassment of pious riches. As in all convents there is a blending of smells: floor-polish, brass-polish, incense and wax (coming from one direction), cooking (coming from the opposite direction). So strong is the force of association that I now, after visits to many convents, find this composite smell vaguely uplifting rather than, as at first, disagreeable and depressing. I have a feeling it is a smell which convents will eventually grow out of, and that when they do it will mean one more symbol gone. I hope if I live to visit convents as a jubilarian, modernisation will not have caught up quite so far.

During this past week I have learned quite a lot about Reverend Mother, and I have met the egregious Gum. Since Gum is likely to loom large upon my horizon while I am stationed up here he must be given more than casual mention. I do not know either of them well enough yet to judge, but from what I have seen of the two in action I recognise a certain affinity. For one thing they use the same sort of terms when alluding to one another: old rogue, old ruffian, old rascal. Reverend Mother was right about Gum being frank. What he lacks in respect for his employers he makes up for in forthrightness of speech.

A word, then, about this Gum. He must be about fifty, so a good twenty years junior to Reverend Mother (who speaks of him as of someone nearing the grave), and is always unshaved. His shaving must be like the jam for tea in *Alice*: yesterday and tomorrow. He shuffles about in brown shoes without any laces. His clothes hang from him as though there were weights in the turn-ups of his trousers, in the lower pockets of his several waistcoats, and in the seams of his oil-stained sports coat. His face and figure sag too. He wears a cloth cap inside the house and out, and when he pushes it back from his forehead with a hot forearm it droops along with the rest. To look at him you would say that Gum was a soft, idle, dreary man. But you would be wrong. He is possessed of enormous strength, an appetite for work, and a vein of humour which is characteristic. I have it only on hearsay that he is strong and hardworking, but from the nature of our introduction I deduce his lighter side. He was lying under the convent lorry when I saw him first. His head was hidden from me, as was mine from him, and since the engine was running it was no time for cosy civilities. Seeing my legs as I was passing he shouted over the rattle, 'Just you 'op in a minute, mate, and press down the accelerator . . . only gently to start off.' I did as requested, and when at last the motor was satisfying the mechanic with its measured burr I heard coming up from underneath: 'Throb, throb, throb . . . like the 'uman 'eart in bliss or deepest anguish.' Then he wriggled out, wiped his hands on the tumbling slack of his many garments, and asked if I could lend him half a crown to have his hair cut. Since this meeting, we have several times exchanged greetings. I have not yet reached the stage of calling him Gum, but am confident that the day is not far off. For his part he addresses me neither as Father nor Sir, an omission which I do not resent. 'Yer 'arf crown's coming back to yer, mate, first thing out of the pay packet.' Perhaps a shade familiar for a handy-man, but I am perhaps a shade pompous for a priest.

From observation, as well as hearing what people have had to tell me about her, I have increased my knowledge of Reverend Mother. I have been in to see her on most days after class, and on each occasion she has lectured me on how to teach. But where another might have been tiresome about it, Reverend Mother has imparted a good deal of wisdom without seeming to treat me as a child. Her information service must be efficient because she knows what I am teaching over at the school almost as soon as the classes end. 'You are not as interested in catechism are you, Father,' she said the other day, putting a king of clubs on a queen of diamonds, 'as in holy scripture?'

'I am afraid not, Reverend Mother.'

'They tell me you have unexpected interpretations of events in scripture, and they like this. Have you no unexpected interpretations of the answers in the catechism?'

'It sounds a risky idea to me. I can hardly take a chance on dogma. What would you say if I made a mistake, Reverend Mother?'

'You are making mistakes anyway, Father, and I would

rather you made a mistake out of zeal than out of caution.'

'I have got zeal all right, Reverend Mother.'

'I wonder if you have. Zeal and wanting results are not the same thing.'

So she is obviously perceptive, sometimes acerbic, always single-minded. Her desire to provide the best for these children shows up in every conversation we have, and I can well understand why the children flock to her in their free time. She stands no nonsense from them, but she is more human with them than with the nuns. I suspect that the nuns bore her a little. She clearly enjoys breaking a lance with Gum, and I imagine that the milder kind of duel which she has with me is stimulating to her, but with the boys and girls she is apparently mother, aunt, friend and confidant. With them she is said to laugh; with the rest of us she never gets beyond an amused chuckle. To the nuns she may be the matriarch but I doubt if she is the mother. From the priests with whom I am living I understand that she is pretty generally feared in the neighbourhood. The parents are afraid of her blunt attacks on their irresponsibility, the staff say she is a martinet, the servants stay out of her way. Gum is the only one, they tell me, who stands up to her. 'If you manage to get on with her,' one of the priests said to me, 'either she is changing or you are.' (The priest in question had known me when I was at school.)

Now that she has recovered from her lumbago, Reverend Mother is getting about. Having seen her only sitting down I was amazed to discover how small she is. The air of command had led me to expect someone taller. On her feet she is as imperious as in a chair, but the fact that for some reason she wears gymshoes does not help in the matter of height. Black gymshoes. Perhaps as our friendship ripens she will tell me why. If she does not, Gum will.

In case I have not sufficiently described Reverend Mother I might add here that she is neither thin nor fat but has good bones. Her nose is long, slender, and straight; her cheekbones are high and pronounced; her hands are well modelled, and, though clearly the hands of an old lady, unspoiled by rheumatism. She holds herself very straight, leaning forward only to glare at an antagonist. Here where everyone speaks with the north-country accent, it is refreshing to hear Reverend

Mother and Gum talking to one another in voices quite different. Gum is unmistakably from London. Reverend Mother's is not a regional accent: it is the inherited accent which belongs by right and not by cultivation to the older English families. Her choice of words is often unexpected, but my guess is that she puts this on. I do not mean that she wants to impress me or anyone else, but simply that to round off a carefully constructed speech with a phrase which is almost slang amuses her. She is a stylist, and her particular style is to mix the colloquial with the formidable. What the north-country lay-men and the Irish sisters make of this I do not know, but it is probably one of the things which delight the children.

As unexpected as the gymshoes is Reverend Mother's disregard of time. It is not that she becomes tedious after a while — she never becomes that — but that she has no sense of urgency. The sisters take it in turns, and are ordered by her to do so, to fetch her for the Office in choir and for meals. She is late for appointments, and when she has to make a journey which does not involve being met at the other end it seems that she prefers to go when she feels like it to the station or bus-stop and wait. 'I see no attraction in punctuality,' she told me yesterday when I jumped up at the sound of the school bell. Such indifference must be a rare quality among women superiors. The admission reminded me of the unopened letters piled high on her desk which I noticed in the early days of my association with St Bride's. It is said that though she gets up regularly at the call every morning, she goes to bed at all hours. I asked her how she managed to run the place without a more fixed method, and how she could be sure of getting in the stipulated periods of prayer and spiritual reading. 'By never carrying a watch,' was her answer.

'It is a great advantage,' she elaborated, 'in supervising an establish-ment of this size that the head should not always be where you expect it to be. You may have noticed that I have no telephone. Nor do I employ a system of communication within the house. If people want to see me they have to look for me; if I want to see people I have to go and find them. It makes for flexibility on both sides. Efficiency and regimentation would save a good deal of time, I grant you that, and perhaps save a certain amount of money as well. But there are more important things than time and money. It is my experience that prayer and study suffer more from anxiety about time and method than from interruption and adaptation.'

Gum owns a cat. He also owns two daughters whom I teach on five mornings a week. It is to the cat and not the daughters that Reverend Mother takes objection. It is not an attractive cat, but Gom likes it and it is certainly attached to Gum. 'If I ever see that cat of yours inside the convent,' I heard Reverend Mother say this morning through one of the windows of the connecting corridor to Gum, who was unloading crates from a van, 'I'll wring its neck.'

Without so much as a glance in the direction of the speaker, and also without a smile or a pause, Gum bent down and said to his cat: 'You 'eard what that nice kind lady's been saying, my sweet one, and if you're thinking the same as me it's what a truly Christian 'eart she must 'ave.'

It seemed to me unlikely that Reverend Mother would continue the conversation. But if I was mentally counting her out I underestimated her powers of recovery.

'Since you have thought well to bring Christianity into this, Gum,' she said, hugely enjoying herself but betraying none of it, 'you should know that nowhere in the New Testament does the mention of a cat occur. And don't you tell me that you made a mistake and were thinking of the Old Testament. That won't do either. The word "cat" appears only once in the Old Testament – in the Prophecy of Baruch if you want to look it up – and it is by no means certain that the sacred writer was referring to the cat as we know the animal today.'

All Gum had to say in answer to this, and again addressed to the cat, was, 'We'll bet he was.'

When I joined Reverend Mother indoors I congratulated her on winning the round. 'Round?' she said. 'Oh yes, boxing. But if he's in his corner now, he won't be there for long. But I had him against the ropes with that bit about Baruch didn't you think? You see, I looked up 'cat' beforehand, in Crudden's, because I knew the information would come in useful sooner or later.'

'And you have the nerve to tell me, Reverend Mother, that you are unsystematic and cannot work to a method.'

'Touchée,' she said, and added quickly 'though that's the wrong term if we are still talking of the ring.'

'How would you like to teach church history for the rest of the term instead of catechism?' Reverend Mother asked me one day last week.

'I don't know any,' I answered.

'You don't know any theology either, and I have a feeling that if you studied the history of the Church you would come to see how the theology of the Church developed from century to century.'

'I see exactly what you are getting at, Reverend Mother,' I said; 'by the end of the term I shall find I have been teaching church history *and* catechism. As well as scripture. I'm not on.'

'It puzzles me that you, a reasonably well-informed and pious priest —' I bowed and put on the kind of face which a reasonably well-informed and pious priest might be expected to wear when he is being wheedled into doing something which he does not want to do — 'should be so devoid of interest in dogma. My spies tell me, Father, that your treatment of death, purgatory, hell and heaven this morning was well below standard. The children who looked in at break, just after you had been teaching them, were full of what you had said about death. They liked that. But they couldn't remember what you had said about purgatory, hell, and heaven.'

'What I said was —'

'Oh, don't bother to tell me, Father. I am sure it was straight out of the book and perfectly orthodox. At least you didn't tell them to try to *imagine,* one by one, the four last things. That might have excited them but it would have told them nothing. As far as it went what you told them was all right. It is just that, apart from the bit about death, I doubt if you believed half of it.'

'Reverend Mother,' I protested. But she swept on.

'Don't misunderstand me. You *accept* the Church's teaching on these four last things but you feel only one of them as a reality. If all four were real to you — if in *that* sense you believed in them — the children would have remembered what you said about them. Anyway I am glad you confined yourself to four last things and didn't give them a fifth to worry about — limbo.'

69

'I thought I would leave limbo till next time. If I am to answer questions about it, I must get it up thoroughly.'

'I shouldn't if I were you. Skip it altogether unless someone asks. Personally I have the greatest difficulty in believing that there is such a place – or such a state or such a necessity – as limbo. I suppose you would call me a heretic. Or, if you are in a generous mood, half a heretic.'

'It does rather surprise me. Myself I have always taken limbo for granted – together with everything else.'

'So you are orthodox, and I am not. Don't let me sow the seeds of doubt in your mind about limbo. But in your charity leave me with my little heresy. I sometimes think that the not absolutely orthodox are safer in the long run than the romantics like yourself. It is often the enthusiasts, who never question a single point of doctrine, that leave the Church while hardboiled old sceptics like myself stick on. I trust a realist; I'm not sure that I always trust a romantic.'

The convent is in a great state of excitement because Mother General, a Frenchwoman, is paying a visit next week. They call it an unofficial visit, a purely domestic affair, but to judge from the preparations that are being made it looks as though it will prove an occasion of high and public celebration. November seems an odd time to choose, but perhaps Mother General has had the wisdom to steer clear of prize-givings and the greater feasts of the Church. They say she has no English. It will be interesting to see if Reverend Mother, our Reverend Mother, exchanges her gymshoes for something more formal. I am also wondering if Gum, who is bound to appear in one or other capacity, will appear shaved. The air is charged with speculation.

'It is no good asking me what day or time Mother General is arriving,' I was told when I called to see if we would be let off classes in honour of the visit, 'you know I have no interest in details of that sort. I have had the best room made ready for her, and when she comes she comes. I was her novice mistress at the mother house and I love her dearly – better than almost anyone – but if there's one thing I dislike it's fuss. You may have noticed that most nuns love fuss, and especially Mother-General fuss. The sisters pretend they want everything done simply, but in fact they want to get all the excitement out of it they can. They tell me I should ask the Bishop but I'm not going to. There's nothing like a bishop for spoiling the fun. Inevitably he divides the interest. You will enjoy watching the kind of high-jinks we'll go in for when Mother General alights among us. What weddings and triumphal victories in the sporting world are to men and women outside, visits from Mother General are to us.'

'Debarred from champagne and party clothes,' I said, 'you must be restricted to music, flowers, and speeches.'

'At this time of the year to music and speeches. Perhaps it's just as well that most flowers are out of season. For the feast of St Patrick the sisters dye white carnations green, and it seems such a shame that an expensive and really rather pretty flower should be made to look like a salad.'

Gum came into the room just then – the door being half open as usual – and Reverend Mother sent him out again. 'Knock when you want to see me, Gum; I have told you about this before.' Gum backed across the threshold, closed the door, and then administered the kind of blow which an auctioneer's hammer might have given to the desk before an assembly of deaf bidders. 'Come in, Gum, come in. But you know you haven't got it quite right yet. The idea is to warn the occupant of the room that further privacy cannot be counted upon: it is not to break down a barricade. Say for instance I am alone with my thoughts, or doing something to my teeth, or listening to birdsong as it comes in through the window, I do not want to be startled out of my wits by what might be the report of a rifle. Remember this another time. Now Gum –' folding her hands one over the other on the table in front of her – 'what was it you wished to consult me about?'

'May I speak freely in front of Father?' asked Gum. I of course got to my feet – as Gum had clearly intended that I should – and was making for the door when Reverend Mother called me back.

'No disclosures can shock Father. Years of practice in the confessional –' I am twenty-seven and was ordained two years ago – 'have rendered him virtually immune. Speak out like a man, Gum, I'm waiting.'

'Do you want the platform put up in the gym,' asked Gum in a voice heavy with deference, 'or is the Right Reverend Mother General of the Order just going to take us as she finds us?'

When Gum had left the room, with instructions to set up the platform as for the most ceremonial of occasions, I said I thought he had worked up to his anticlimax rather skilfully.

'Not at all,' said Reverend Mother, 'he didn't deceive me for a moment. I can't think why you have a good word to say for him. He's a brigand. Has he given you back your half-crown?'

'Not yet. I like Gum, Reverend Mother. I like his snarling good nature, and the despair in his upward look to heaven when you tell him to do anything. If he is a rogue and a brigand it is because you encourage him.'

'He's an old rascal. Don't you trust him an inch.'

I have just come from the convent after attending the formal welcome given to Mother General by the community, staff, and school of St Bride's. If I do not write it all down at once I may forget, and the occasion is worth recording. The first thing that emerges pretty clearly is that Reverend Mother has misled me about her indifference to detail. Today's performance must have been planned with the exactitude of an army manoeuvre, and it went off without a hitch. This time yesterday it seemed unlikely that anything would be ready and that the programme which had been arranged could possibly be realised. For the past three days confusion had been mounting steadily, and everywhere one heard 'Where's Reverend Mother? . . . ask Reverend Mother . . . I'll see Reverend Mother about it . . . don't put it there in case Reverend Mother . . . there's a message for Reverend Mother about the hired chairs . . . about the tea for the guests . . . about where the photographs are to be taken.'

Not having any part in the work of preparation I amused myself in forecasting delays here and accidents there. But I have been shown up wrong on every count. Even in the last-minute race after breakfast this morning to pin up WELCOME TO REVEREND MOTHER GENERAL high on the gymnasium wall no sister fell, as I had prophesied, from a ladder into a waiting bucket; no tethered rope became unfastened, as I had foreseen, to lash an upturned face. Each sister had her appointed task, and the bustle was orderly. Carpets were tacked to the boards so as to guard against the tripping foot;

72

pots of evergreens were pushed against Gum's platform with the smooth precision of a naval tattoo; children, scrubbed and pink and holding in their hands the score from which they were to sing *In dulce jubilo*, were marshalled into an improvised pen reserved for the choir. Then parents, guests, hangers-on like me who are loosely connected with the place, the two hundred children of the school and a handful of diocesan clergy streamed in. Except for the central aisle, coconut-matted, leading from the door to the steps of the platform, the gymnasium was packed. We all had our programmes, and there was that low buzz which is like the sound of many skaters on ice when heard from a distance. At three minutes to the hour (and I reminded myself that Reverend Mother scorns a watch) the community filed in, thirty strong, and took up a stand at the back of the platform leaving plenty of space in front — so much space indeed that for one hopeful moment I wondered if Mother General would be coming on horseback. In their white habits, fresh from the laundry and the iron, the sisters made the rest of us look shabby and crumpled. The expressions on their faces ranged over a variety of emotions: reminiscence (the older ones had been through all this before and were thinking of Mothers General long dead), demure recollection, weariness ('all this tomfoolery when there is work to be done and no time to do it in'), condescension, quiet enjoyment, frank excitement.

With the clock above the wall-bars showing eleven precisely, the double doors drew back to admit Reverend Mother and her guest of honour. Only when I had looked to see what Reverend Mother was wearing on her feet — and I was glad to note that she was making no concession to the grandeur of the occasion — did I study Mother General's appearance. She is a tall and smiling woman, very different from her one-time novice mistress, with a high complexion and a line of soft dark down on the upper lip. The two moved briskly over the width of coconut matting between the crowd of clapping, rather hot, over-dressed, spectators. The platform reached, Reverend Mother raised a hand and at once there was complete silence. It was as though an engine had been suddenly turned off. Or rather it was as though a silent engine had been turned on.

In fluent and conversational French, with nothing of the set

73

speech about it and with no notes, Reverend Mother said in effect how jolly it was to be able to entertain her superior in this way and that she wished it could happen more often. She spoke briefly of Mother General's work for the Order, of the weight she carried with the higher clergy (laughter from those who wanted to show that they knew French), and of her particular affection for the English convents. Then, careful to give the key word in English, Reverend Mother said she had asked Sister Lioba to arrange for a holiday in Mother General's honour. If they had understood nothing else of the address, the children managed to understand this — and roared their appreciation accordingly. Silence again, followed by a boring speech in French by Mother General. Then came *In dulce jubilo*, a few practical remarks and statistics from Sister Lioba, and a few minutes devoted to photography. By way of tying up the ceremony, a bouquet of hothouse flowers and an album of school prints were presented by the youngest child. The usual, and to me always painfully uncomfortable, three cheers. Then down from the platform and out. At the door everyone who had been present was given a card which on one side showed a picture of Mother Foundress in her black veil and white habit (and below it a prayer for her beatification), on the other the words TO REMIND YOU OF THE OCCASION OF MOTHER GENERAL'S VISIT TO ST BRIDE'S, 15th NOVEMBER 1932.

'You must be glad it's all over,' I said to Reverend Mother when her superior had left for Ireland on her way back to France.

'Extremely. But I like Mother General: she has all my nice qualities without any of my compensating drawbacks. She stands no nonsense — sweetly.' She dealt out her cards for a new patience.

'Her visit was a great success. She will have been impressed.'

'Where did you hide, by the way? I wanted you to be introduced, but perhaps your French would not have been equal to it. You could have exchanged pleasantries in Latin, Greek, or Hebrew. She's weak on modern languages but as likely as not says the rosary in Aramaic. You did not meet her then?'

'I mix uneasily with the great. I am more at home with old friends like Gum. I looked out for Gum during the celebrations, but couldn't find him. Wasn't he there — after all the work he had put into it?'

'Ah Gum. No, he wasn't there. Gum is in the unfortunate position of having, every now and again, to take a sabbatical. Not a sabbatical year, of course, but just four or five days off. Poor old Gum.' She sighed, and made small clicking noises with her mouth in the way that patience-players are accustomed to do. But since she had hardly got going on her patience I wondered whether it might not be the thought of Gum that was occupying her mind. 'All that work of preparing for Mother General's visit was too much for him. Bowled him over.'

'You mean he drinks?'

'Not sip, sip, sip. Just once every six weeks or so. Not a cork drawn for a considerable time, then *pop* and the old villain is oblivious of the passage of time until he crawls in here, usually without knocking, to apologise. I blame myself sometimes for giving him too much to do.' This last sentence was spoken in an almost gruff undertone. 'But perhaps if I gave him too little,' she sighed, 'I would have to blame myself even more.'

'Gum, what do you think you're doing up there? Come down at once.'

The speaker was within earshot but not within my range of vision. Nor could I see Gum, but it was nice to know that his sabbatical was over.

'Looking for strawberries. Anything I can do for you while I'm waiting for 'em to grow?'

Gum was lying on the flat roof over the sacristy, clearing a rain-pipe of packed and frozen snow. Catching sight of me when I came to see what these two were up to, Reverend Mother addressed her next commands in my direction.

'Kindly ask Sister Joanna to bring out the mats from under the beds in the infirmary. Tell her I want them on the sacristy roof. If that old idiot spends much longer on his stomach in the snow he'll kill himself. I don't want to be had up for neglect of those under my charge.'

I did as I was told, and Gum, who had heard Reverend Mother's words, accepted the mats without either gratitude or protest. It was far too cold to wait and see whether or not Gum, from an uncomfortable angle, would be able to dislodge enough snow to make the rain-pipes usable, so Reverend Mother and I, our feet crunching and squeaking over the snow (she was wearing wellingtons *on top of*, as she told me, her gymshoes) walked back together to the convent.

'He's not a bad fellow,' I said, 'and what's more, Reverend Mother, you know it.'

'Gum?' she said, banging the boots on the step to get rid of the snow. 'A man of unsleeping malevolence.' I tried to see her face but it was hidden from me as she bent over the job in hand.

We are now in December, and this is probably the last entry I shall make in this record of my time in the north. The term ends next week but before that I am due to move south; back to the monastery. Reverend Mother asked me to say Mass today in the convent, which I did. Any children who wanted to were allowed to come for it, and of course all the nuns were there. I do not know what either the children or the sisters felt during Mass, but I was strangely moved. At breakfast afterwards there were cards and notes and little presents on the table. After breakfast Reverend Mother came in for a few minutes alone. She looked smaller than ever; perhaps it is the cold. She also looks older, but this may be because she is wearing a woollen shawl. Also I have noticed that old people tend to look older in the reflected light of the snow. Today the sun is shining and the air indoors is clear; the light is almost green.

'In a minute I am going to take you out to say goodbye to the community. I shall not be there for that. So I say goodbye now. May I have your blessing?' I gave it. 'Don't order a taxi to take you to the station from the priest's house. Gum wants to take you. See that he gives you your half-crown. You may like to know that with Sister Lioba's approval I have allowed the children whom you have been teaching, those two forms, to have a free morning in your honour. Some of them may perhaps go to the station to see you off.'

This was said in such a dry matter-of-fact voice that I could not well alter the tone of the interview by introducing a warmer note. I wanted to show gratitude but did not know how to without sounding sentimental.

'I hope they will,' I said instead. And then, making conversation against the moment when I would have to say goodbye to the sisters, I added: 'I did not know that in a state-aided school you could grant holidays like this. It puzzled me when you granted a holiday in honour of Mother General's visit: I meant to ask you but forgot. Couldn't the authorities come down on you for it?'

'I'd like to see them try.'

THAT NICE SPY

It was under U.S. military auspices. I was to give a series of what they called 'one-day stands' in the American sector of Germany. It meant that at each of the appointed stopping-places down the Rhine, ending up in Munich at the barracks which had been General Patton's head-quarters, I was to say Mass, preach three times, hear confessions, and appear on the platform to answer questions. The itinerary had been worked out in minutest detail. Weeks before the time of starting I was getting passes which would be valid when military transport was not provided, information as to where and when and by whom I would be met, hotel reservations when not accommodated by one or other of the services, and even a list of addresses to be consulted in the event of failure to connect. It was this last which should have put me on my toes.

On January 2nd, 1955, I set out in a U.S. forces plane from London to Frankfurt. The time at which I was to be met by a Major Saslec at Frankfurt Airport was given as 14.20 hours. At 16.20 hours we landed at Brussels Airport, and I sent a telegram to Major Saslec which cost me ten shillings in English money because it was the only money I had. Boarding the same plane (I was the one civilian) we must then have traced an interesting course over a quite large area of Europe because it was after midnight by the time we touched down, in a blizzard, at Frankfurt.

The ground personnel on night duty in German airports is, anyway so far as the female staff are concerned, divided sharply into two groups. You have the twinkling helpful kind who appear in the coloured advertisements and who speak eagerly to you in an enchanting mixture of Manhattan and Hamburg, and you have the hard-eyed disillusioned kind who, if they can possibly help it, do not speak to you at all. My lot, early in the morning of January 3rd, fell among the second kind. Whether it was my civilian status or my British nationality that went against me I do not know, but the girl at the desk was hostile. No R.T.O. or his equivalent appeared to be on hand, no buses were leaving the airport until six, and there was no hotel. I asked if a message had come for me. The girl shook her head without bothering to look. The available armchairs were occupied by American servicemen, Negro and white, while on some benches against the wall sat crumpled German civilians whose function I was not able to determine. There were about twenty in all: some asleep, some listlessly reading yesterday's papers, some drinking coffee and smoking, all of them silent and waiting for the world to end.

Consulting my list of emergency enquiry centres, a list which I was to make good use of during the next ten days, I asked the girl at the desk if I might use her telephone. She did not understand. I repeated the question in German. She understood but shook her head. Just to see what would happen, I asked her in French. She did not even shake her head; she glared. My knowledge of languages had run out, but since I had no intention of hunting for a telephone-box at one in the morning I picked up the receiver and withdrew as far from the counter as the flex allowed. Whereupon my opponent seized the telephone itself and clasped it to her breast. Wolves howling for the infant, *tu ne passes pas,* curfew shall not ring tonight. In my stupidity I had overlooked the necessity of dialling the number I wanted, so the situation appeared to have reached a deadlock from which neither of us could retreat without serious loss of face.

At this point one of the crumpled men on the bench, all of whom I had taken to be Germans, got up and came over to me. His walk was unmistakably English.

'The redcoats have got through,' said a rather donnish voice; 'the position, God willing, can be righted.'

In rapid German the crumpled man, while gently taking the telephone away from the girl and the receiver from me, issued instructions. Part general, part conjurer. From his bench he had evidently heard the salient points of the discussion because in no time at all an envelope with my name on it was produced, the message inside being from Major Saslec welcoming me to Frankfurt and enclosing a key to his apartment ('that means "flat" ' my new friend explained), and a chit made out promising me transportation ('that means a car') to Frankfurt within twenty minutes. Furnished so suddenly and unexpectedly with everything necessary, I turned with gratitude to my benefactor. Not only with gratitude but with wonderment.

Crumpled is less than the truth. He could hardly have presented a more tumbledown appearance. An untended moustache like a broken comb, a two days' growth of beard, greying hair sweeping his ears, lines across his forehead and down his fleshless cheeks. I put him down as fifty; anyway not much less. His clothes were downhill too, but whereas his face had been something at one time his dress had never aspired high. He was wearing an old battledress blouse, dyed blue, grey twill trousers, brown canvas tennis-shoes such as I had not seen for years and believed were no longer made, spotted silk scarf tucked into a frayed green pullover. In his hand he held a beret, and since he carried no luggage I assumed he was employed at the airport. But whatever his employment he was difficult to place. My first thought was that he must be a deserter. But why would a man desert from the British Army into the American sector where it would be easy to trace him? A spy perhaps. But with his voice he was giving himself away to every listener. He did not strike me as a beachcomber, an airport bum. I would be more able to tell if he asked for money. Or if on the other hand he gave me a letter of introduction to Chancellor Adenauer. While I was speculating he was talking. He was going on about the girl at the desk.

'Lisa's not like that as a rule; something must be biting her. I'll get her mother to talk to her. Great chaps for the family, these Germans.'

'Night duty can't be much fun,' I conceded, 'but you would have thought someone who could understand English would be given the job.'

'She speaks it perfectly.'

By this time a big grey car with a white star on the door had drawn up and the driver was taking my suitcase and typewriter.

'Mind if I join you? I've got things to do in Frankfurt later on in the morning.'

'Of course, do.'

I was glad of his company on the long drive which took us first through snow-covered forests and then past luminous fields. The blizzard had quite suddenly stopped, leaving the country exhausted and white. The suburb came upon us as though dropped by accident out of a child's box of bricks, quick contrast to the rural scene, and the driver, who was known to my companion, had no difficulty in finding the street where Major Saslec lived. It was now getting on for three. My companion, who had kept up a flow of amusing monologue throughout the drive, seemed to grow less crumpled as the night wore on. He still gave no inkling as to his profession; nor did he tell me if he was a Catholic, whether he was married or single, what his story had been in England. In fact though he talked a lot he told me nothing.

'I'll just see you in,' he said as we stood on the doorstep, 'and the chuvver had better go back to bed. Goodnight, Al, and don't give lifts to unauthorised persons while in charge of a service vehicle.'

'Okay, Captain. Be seeing you.'

The apartment building which housed Major Saslec was of the kind which, while proposing minimum trouble to the many, gives maximum trouble to the few. You ring at the outside door; the porter or landlord or concierge then rings back; you push, and the door opens three inches until it comes up against a brass chain; while you are wondering what the next move is, the door swings purposefully back and locks itself. Then you begin all over again, trying to suggest by the tempo of your ringing that the only course open to the porter is to get out of bed and let you in. However many latchkeys you are carrying none is any use until you have got past the first barrier.

After a surprisingly short wait in the snow we heard someone coming, and the chain was lifted. We were greeted not by an indignant porter in his pyjamas but by a fully dressed and happy old lady wearing a henna wig and carrying a jug of hot milk and a French horn. She explained in German that she was the landlady. Since his German was so much better than mine the crumpled man did the talking. No, no, we must not apologise: English visitors were welcome at any time. Lateness of the hour? Not at all; this was a nice quiet time of the day when perhaps we would like to drink hot milk and listen to the French horn. Our hostess then introduced herself formally as Frau Vischling and beamed at us with a set of teeth faintly tinged with blue like a duck's egg.

'I will now play you some calls on the French horn. It is a very beautiful instrument.' She gave a toot on it, and with mugs of hot milk in our hands we sat down. 'Strange, you may think, to hear the French horn in Germany. My late husband, Herr Vischling, feared it might shock. You are not shocked?'

She was assured that we were far from shocked, and that the French horn enjoyed considerable prestige in England. Not at all, sleep was of no concern. But would not the other occupants be disturbed?

'Ah, no. There is the Major Saslec at the top of the house, and he sleeps profoundly. One couple immediately below him, but they are German and the Germans are a musical race. I will now blow you a little piece composed by my late husband, Herr Vischling, especially for the chase.'

At four the crumpled man left the house. Frau Vischling made him take her late husband's overcoat which she said he could return any time he liked or not at all. It was with difficulty that she was prevented from filling a thermos of hot milk for him to take with him. Had he asked for a French horn she might have thought twice but she would have given it to him.

'Give me the time of your train from Frankfurt tomorrow and I'll be there,' he said to me as we shook hands at the door (Frau Vischling was seeing to it that the mechanism which controlled the door did not cut us off prematurely), 'never know; there might be a hitch. In the meantime here's a telephone number which will find me in case anything goes wrong.'

As it turned out my departure from Frankfurt proved one of the few occasions on the tour when there was no hitch. The time between getting to bed and completing the 'one-day stand' allowed few gaps, so I did not in fact telephone. It was as much as I could do to get through the duties lined up for me. Fortunately I could count on Major Saslec, who revealed himself to be a competent, kindly, and humorous guide. Since Mass was to be in the evening – the first, and up till now the only, time I have not said Mass in the morning – I met my host at a conveniently late breakfast before my opening discourse. Quiet, young, sandy-haired, soft-spoken, Major Saslec won my affection at the first blush of the tomato-juice.

'I hope you had no difficulty getting in last night?'

'None. Your charming landlady let us in. I arrived with a man I met at the airport. Frau Vischling treated us to a blast or two on the French horn.'

'Ah, then her teeth were in.'

'Row upon row. Does she not normally include them?'

'She values them solely as a buttress to the mouthpiece of the French horn. She has no call to masticate, living the way she does almost exclusively on hot milk.'

Major Saslec drove to the base where I was to speak, introduced me to the great, and generally nannied me. There must be something about me which rouses the mother instinct. I have only to appear looking wretched and people wrap rugs around my knees and bring me something hot to drink. I never cease to give thanks to God.

I delivered my three talks, was hospitably entertained for luncheon in the officers' mess, and was let off lightly on the platform by congenital hecklers who at the last moment felt themselves unaccountably protective. Two enormous G.I.'s, towering above my insular six foot one, and very smart in their white gaiters, served my Mass. I got back to the apartment house only just in time to hear what I supposed was the Last Post on the French horn. ('Not the Last Post but Lights Out,' Major Saslec corrected me later, 'though as far as I can figure it she herself keeps the lights on all night.')

Major Saslec served my Mass in the morning at the parish church, took me back to the house to collect my things and say goodbye to Frau Vischling, and drove me to the station. I looked everywhere for the crumpled man, partly because I thought he and Major Saslec would enjoy one another and partly because I hoped the crumpled man was as good as his word and that I would see him again, but there was no sign of him.

Even after so short a visit I was sorry to be leaving Frankfurt.

'I'd forgotten they would send you first class,' said the crumpled man as he pulled back the door of the compartment, 'I was pigging it at the other end.'

'How good of you to come,' I said, faintly embarrassed, 'I thought you must have changed your mind.' I try never to show surprise, even to my nearest and dearest. 'I wanted you to meet the chap who was seeing me off, Major Saslec. Nice chap.'

'That was just it. I like to know beforehand whom I'm meeting, and I hadn't come across this Saslec. So I did a bunk. I don't think he can have been here long.'

'I have no idea. He didn't tell me.' The spy idea had come back to me. I had put it away as if it was a letter from a tiresome nun.

'You mean you didn't ask? Of course not – why should you? Tell me, how was the old lady's wig when you saw it last? Jollier by daylight?'

'Worse. Unripe beetroot.'

'I was afraid it would be. Well, I'm getting off at Stuttgart so the time has almost come for parting. Our beautiful friendship is drawing to a close.'

'May I pay your fare? They threw me a purse of gold at the U.S. base last night, so I won't be out of pocket.'

'To look at me you might not think I was rich beyond the dreams of avarice. Nevertheless I want for nothing. Keep your dollar-marks for the Abbot. Now what time does that itinerary sheet say we reach Stuttgart? Because I must get back to the cattle-trucks and galleys.'

As I drew the sheaf of papers from my pocket the train gave a metallic hiccup, and two of the pages fell to the floor. It was as though my clumsiness were a signal. The crumpled man stood up, placed one arm behind his neck and the other stiffly to his side, leaned his head so that the side of his face rested on one raised shoulder, and said this: 'Pick it up, boy, will you, pick it up. Come on, van Zeller, you juggins, this isn't a paper chase, will you.'

'The Bye,' I cried, 'you're doing the Bye.' Thirty years spun back on the time-spool and I was back at school in classroom eight. It was maths on Tuesdays, Thursdays, and Saturdays at 11.50 and the Bye, with his leather face and cotton-wool hair, was taking us for it. I recognised the crumpled man now: he was the little boy in front who was a lot brighter than the rest of us old lags at the back who had already been in the form for a year.

I gripped him by both arms, my boast of never showing surprise flung to the winds. 'But why on earth didn't you let on earlier?' I asked, 'and how did you recognise me? Do you know we haven't met since 1923?'

'I heard you give your name at the airport. Why didn't I let on?

Oh I don't know. Perhaps because I know my place. I was a fag, remember, when you were a school prefect. There used to be a code about these things, though I doubt if they keep it up at Downside now. Besides I rather enjoy playing a part. As, I think, you do too.'

The train was slowing down at Stuttgart.

I have not met him since, nor heard of him. But a year ago at Christmas I received an envelope bearing a Moroccan stamp. It contained, wrapped in tissue paper but without an accompanying message, a doll's wig — red.

PORTRAIT OF AN ANGRY MAN

It is, of course, not at all unusual to find that a name heard for the first time, thereafter keeps cropping up so often and from such different quarters as to make the hearer wonder how he had managed never to hear it before. The mention of Humphrey Jesse was for me a case in point. Until a certain day in November, when I happened to be lunching with two friends in London, I had never heard of the man whom I am here calling Humphrey Jesse. My two friends were actors, and the place where we lunched was the Garrick Club.

There were few people lunching there that day — perhaps November marks a slack season in the stage year — and my hopes that some celebrities might be pointed out to me seemed unlikely to be realised.

'Anyway that's Humphrey Jesse over there, the one eating by himself near the window,' said Eric, one of my hosts, casually, rather as he would have tossed a grilled leg of peacock to a sniffing hound had he been playing a Tudor nobleman. 'You must have heard of him because he's always in the news.'

'And since he's not in anything at the moment,' said Godfrey, 'you are probably seeing him in the last hour of the day when he's more or less sober.'

'The name is new to me,' I admitted. 'Tell me about him.'

It seemed that, if not as famous on the English stage as some of the great ones of his time — the names of Cedric Hardwick, Robert Newton, Charles Laughton, Ralph Richardson were mentioned — Humphrey Jesse was eminent enough to head the list of a supporting cast. It seemed also that he was not liked in the profession, that his aggressiveness made rehearsals uncomfortable for everyone, and that his style of living was doing no good to his career. He was more often seen in films than in plays, and I gathered that this was because nightly performances over a long run would have put too much of a strain upon others besides himself.

So across the dining-room I studied Mr Humphrey Jesse. He was a big man, but powerful rather than gross; florid but not unhealthily so. In an earthy sort of way he might have been called even handsome. Though his expression was disagreeable, and rather suggested he might butt anyone who got in his way, there was still a certain distinction about him. He looked somebody; not just an actor who wanted to look somebody. He must have been about fifty. His hair was grey and thick, his eyebrows prominent, and he was the only man in the room with a moustache. The moustache was as carefully groomed as the rest of him, brushed up like the hair over his ears and the frowning eyebrows. Had I been asked in a paper-and-pencil game to put down three adjectives to describe his appearance I would have written 'hairy, angry, masculine'. A competitor with fewer obligations towards charity might have substituted 'brutal' for one of them.

'He can certainly act,' said Eric in conclusion to his brief character sketch.

'In his own sort of part he can,' Godfrey conceded, 'when all he has to do is walk on and be himself. The German staff officer, the Roman centurian, the brigadier.'

'Look at him now: he's being rude to the nicest of club waiters. I'd say he was the most unpopular member here.'

'Easily,' Godfrey agreed.

I switched my attention from Jesse to the waiter. It came to me that the waiter was neither intimidated nor resentful so much as grieved, and this, if I was right in my guess, gave me pause.

'If it were merely a question of theatrical temperament,' said Eric, 'such as we are all expected to suffer from, it wouldn't matter so much. The trouble is he smoulders, erupts, and then goes on smouldering. He's a man of – ' here Eric put on his Noel Coward voice – 'cantankerous temper, unflinching and dedicated.'

'I'm sorry there's nobody else to show you. Just one person, and not a very charming one at that,' said Godfrey.

'The waiter was charming,' I said.

Next day I was in Sussex, opening a three-day retreat at a boy's school, and rather to my surprise I was told by the headmaster that it was the custom to have a film when the retreat was over (the lump of sugar to follow the castor oil) and that I had better stay for it.

'It's not much of a film,' the headmaster said, 'but there's a chap in it who's very good: a man called Humphrey Jesse who plays the part of a Scots laird on trial for the murder of a poacher.'

I was not able to stay for the film, but was sorry for the poacher.

Not long after this I read in some paper that a well-known actress and television personality was getting a divorce from her husband, Mr Humphrey Jesse, whose second marriage had been dissolved three years earlier.

The next victim of Mr Jesse's ill humour to receive mention in the press was a policeman. When charged with driving a car while under the influence of drink, Mr Jesse had struck the constable, resisted arrest, and used abusive language. The paper went on to say that Mr Jesse was currently appearing in *Raj*, an adaptation of a Kipling story, and that, while on location in India, he had caused several delays in the shooting on account of disagreements with the director. I got the impression that the papers had underlined the name in red pencil.

But all this is – since we are dealing with a member of the profession – by way of *montage*. The story proper has to do with a train journey from Reading to London in the winter of 1957. I had again been giving a retreat, and was on my way to give another one. There had been an unusually heavy fall of snow in Berkshire, and the electric line to Waterloo was affected. The journey took nearly three hours instead of just over one, and though the country looked very beautiful the passengers grew tired of looking at it.

In the compartment with me as we rolled tentatively out of Reading at eight fifty-five were: a businessman, about whom I remember nothing except that he looked determined (and who can blame him, doing the journey every morning?) not to take any part in what might go on around him; a young woman, whose reading matter proclaimed her to be student and whose troubled expression suggested introversion; an apologetic little woman of uncertain age and origin, who was travelling with several parcels and a suitcase which, from the way she looked at them on the rack, were causing her anxiety; and a mother and son. These last two need some further description.

They were bound for an afternoon performance of a pantomime. This information was given by the little boy for the benefit of the rest of us before we had left the station, and from then onwards it was a question of burning moment as to whether or not the train would reach London in time for the pantomime's opening act. Neither the businessman nor the student was ready to be drawn into this. The woman with the parcels speculated hopefully but was not really interested. In me the mother and son had a better audience, but with the snow still falling and the train still hesitating I was not committing myself. The mother interested me by addressing the child as though he were a grown-up, and the child interested me still more by being very much the little boy and not at all the sophisticated son of an obviously sophisticated mother. On her lap were the *Spectator*, the *New Statesman*, the *Tatler*. He had with him a number of comics and a hardback illustrated copy of *Puss in Boots* (to rub up on the plot before this afternoon?), but he was too excited to look at what he had brought with him. I wondered why these two were not in a first-class carriage; they looked rather grand.

I wondered also what else they were planning to do in London besides the pantomime. The mother was dressed more for a cocktail party than a pantomime: jewellery, orchid, and a hat which she would not have chosen for a train journey unless something special awaited her at the end of it. The boy was not in sweater and sandals either. Nothing stirs curiosity like travel. My conjectures were met when the train sighed to a stop between two stations and the small boy asked for the twentieth time if this meant that the pantomime would have started before their arrival. His mother did not answer. She knew as well as I did that the question would come round again.

'We can miss lunch at Aunt Ada's can't we, Mummy, and go straight there? I don't want any lunch.'

'I do,' said his mother, 'now that I'm all togged up.'

'But Aunt Ada's lunches take such *ages*. Couldn't we get ices in the station and eat them in the taxi?'

'If you're going to eat ices on the coldest day of the year, my friend, I'm not. What do you think the gentleman from Wall's would think of me anyway, looking like this?'

'Looking like what?'

'Clanking with diamonds, which I can't just put in a paper bag. No, I'm afraid we'll have to go to Aunt Ada's, even if we are late for her jamboree.'

'Hell, hell, hell. We'll miss *everything*.'

'Peter, stop it. I'm serious.'

There was a steady whirring noise underneath us, like a grandfather clock taking a deep breath before striking, followed after a moment's silence by a resumption of movement. Behind his *Times* the businessman gave no sign that he had heard a word of this exchange; the girl with the textbooks maintained the fixed expression of one who is listening avidly but who does not want to be suspected of doing so; the parcels lady winced at the mention of hell but showed by her sweet smile that allowances must be made for the gentry.

When the train sighed to a snow-cushioned halt at Virginia Water it did so to the accompaniment, on the platform, of a commotion. Two voices could be heard, raised in anger. A railway official was loudly disclaiming responsibility for the snow, for the company's decision to take off the first-class carriages until the power could be strengthened, for any further delays there might be along the line. The other voice — waves of it breaking over the shingle — was making short work of all this.

'Why not look at the rumpus for a bit?' said the mother to the little boy. 'We may be here for some time, and people shouting blue murder at one another are always fun.'

The door of the compartment was wrenched open by the guard and Humphrey Jesse stamped in.

He was even bigger than I remembered him, and well padded out against the cold. Either from the cold or from rage, his face was almost the colour of a plum. One quick glare at his fellow occupants must have convinced him that we were not worth a second look, because the moment he sat down he closed his eyes. He was not trying to go to sleep: he was shutting everything out. He brought no luggage with him, and I noticed that in his large gloved hands he held *The Times Literary Supplement*, the *Connoisseur*, and a French paperback edition of the poems of Tristan Corbière.

It was not difficult to judge the effect of his arrival upon each of our little group. The businessman, pretending not to notice that we had been joined, retreated deeper into the hinterland; the textbook girl gave herself away for a moment by staring, but then decided it would look more dignified if she went back to her studies; the parcels lady shrivelled visibly; the self-possessed mother was amused; the little boy gave the newcomer a steady look of awe.

In the quarter of an hour's delay at Virginia Water nobody spoke. Even the little boy's questions were silenced — by preoccupation. The guard padded along the platform once or twice, self-consciously turning away as he passed our window. Then the whirring began again under our feet, the electricity limbering up, and after the ritual pause the train braved the run once more.

'I say.' It was the little boy's voice, high pitched and clear. He had left his side of the compartment and was standing in front of Jesse whose eyes were still firmly closed. The movement was sudden, and he could not have caused more surprise had he tried to jump out of the window. The rest of us twanged like bow-strings. The businessman brought his paper down as if it had been a starter's flag, looked over the rim of his glasses, and then whisked the paper up again. The girl, too, looked out from her textbooks and was back again. She reminded me of a tortoise. Old parcels pressed her lips together and breathed through her nose.

'I say,' repeated the boy, 'what's your name?'

'Gigglewump,' said Jesse promptly, opening his eyes.

To my great satisfaction, because I thought I knew exactly what was in his mind, the boy did not smile. He did not believe that Jesse's name was Gigglewump any more than the rest of us did, but he did not want to laugh because that would spoil it. It would be like asking what his real name was: once he knew, he would be unable to get back to the promising position he was in now. He did not reason it out like this, but I knew it was what he was thinking. I was trying to think like this myself.

'Tell me a story,' he said gravely.

'Peter, don't be a bore,' said his mother. 'Take your comics and read them in the corridor or in the loo. You'll only annoy people in here.'

Peter ignored this. So did Jesse.

'What sort of a story?'

'Oh, any sort.'

'You're being a pest, Peter,' said his mother.

'We've just had Christmas so it's a bit late for that sort of story,' said Jesse, as if the mother had not spoken, 'and I doubt if you like fairy stories. I'm rather coming round to fairy stories myself.'

'Fairy stories are wet.'

'That's of course the trouble about them. But they are all right if they are frightening, and not strictly about fairies.'

'Yes.'

'I'll tell you a story about a giant who looked like this.'

Jesse ran his hands through his hair so that it stuck out round his head, then stretched his arms high into the air and dropped his hands at the wrist, spreading and curling his fingers so that they looked like claws. He then blew out his cheeks, moustache bristling, and rolled his already rather protruding eyes. It was an image of utmost menace. Peter was enchanted. The preliminary business done, Jesse let his arms drop and folded his hands on his lap. In the course of the story, Peter drew closer and leaned his arms on Jesse's knee. Usually when grown-ups tell stories to children in the presence of other grown-ups they do so with one eye on the adult audience. This was not so here. If Humphrey Jesse gave a thought to the rest of us, it was probably one of loathing. But I doubt if he considered us at all. It was the actor making a selection, and playing accordingly by an appropriate set of rules.

'Only he looked much fiercer because he had a big black beard and one ear higher than the other. He also had craggy teeth and dirty fingernails.'

'What was his name?'

'You're quite right to ask. Names are important. His real name was Giant Blubberguts but his friends called him Tiny. He ate a cow a day, except on his birthday when he ate two, and he kept a python in a tobacco tin.'

'What's a python?'

'A snake which looks like a quiet harmless rubber tube but which crushes people to death. And before you ask what he kept it for I'll tell you; it was for tying knots in when he wanted to remember things.

'Well, one day he got up early, kissed his wife, who was only a few feet smaller than he was, said goodbye to his little giants — each of whom by the way was about the size of a two-storey house — ' Humphrey Jesse used an effective gesture at this and other asides in the story, jerking his hand round his wide front, or pointing a rigid forefinger at his listener's chest — 'and explained about having to attend a meeting of ogres which was due to take place in the mountains. But I am afraid he wasn't telling the truth. All he wanted to do was splash about in a mountain lake which he had seen one day while hunting dragons.

'Now when he jumped into the lake he found that the water overflowed the banks for miles and miles, and this made him laugh because the lake was really quite shallow. It made him feel manly and strong to be able to change the whole countryside by simply sitting down.'

'Were all the people drowned?'

'I'm coming to that. Don't interrupt. The houses and barns started floating about, the people and cattle started swimming for all they were worth, and the little rowing-boats, which the inhabitants used to hire on Sunday afternoons, suddenly became more valuable than the king's palaces and castles. The king doesn't come into the story, so shut up. Only the tops of the very tallest trees showed above the surface of the water. All might have been lost had not a little boy — younger than you, much — been sailing his boat on the lake when the giant had plunged in. Still clutching his boat under his arm, this young man was carried by the wave to the topmost branches of one of these very tall trees for which that country was famous.'

'What was the country called?'

'It's a secret. It doesn't appear on any map. And I said don't interrupt.'

'Here, then, you have the boy hiding in the branches with his sailing-boat while the giant sings away and splashes in the lake which has become a fair-sized sea. The giant is used to children who are enormous, so of course he doesn't see this one although he's looking *straight at the tree*. Seeing the damage he's done, old Blubberguts starts roaring his head off with laughter. "Ha, ha, ha . . . ha, ha, ha." The mountains echo these gales of gigantic laughter.'

The parcels on the rack seemed to tremble, and we were all, even the businessman, watching the performance.

'But sucks to him, because the boy in the tree suddenly has an idea. Leaning very carefully out of the branches like this —' Mr Jesse showed exactly — 'he launches his sailing-boat on the water and gives it a good shove. You can guess what happens: the boat goes sailing straight into the giant's open laughing mouth. The giant coughs and splutters, shakes his head and thumps his chest, holds his ears and pulls outwards so as to loosen the terrible moorings in his throat. No good. He even puts his head under water and comes up blowing spouts of the stuff from his nostrils — like a whale you know — but that's no good either. The boat is firmly lodged somewhere in among his tonsils. "Boo, hoo, hoo . . . boo, hoo, hoo." The mountains echo to these cries of gigantic pain. "Excuse me," said the little boy in a put-on brave voice, "but I think you have got my boat. When you've finished with it, I mean, I'd rather like it back." "Oh, you can have it, you can have it," came the croaky, splodgy, plaintive voice of poor Giant Blubberguts. "*Please* take it away." "Only on twenty-one conditions," said the little boy. "Yech, yech," said the giant, stumbling over his sibilants. "I accthept the lot."

' "The first is that you won't shut your mouth; the second is that you go home quietly to your big family; the third is that you eat no more cows; the fourth is that you say you are sorry; the fifth . . ."

' "Yech, yech, I promich. I acchepth all the other fifteench conditioncth."

'So the little boy walked into the giant's mouth, un-hitched his sailing-boat, and climbed out again. The giant swallowed once or twice to make sure, and then stood up. As soon as he was on his feet again the water subsided, and the lake became a lake again. I should explain that the whole affair was so quick from start to finish that none of the people or animals had had time to drown. All that had happened was that a lot of houses and barns had come down where they hadn't been before. The fields, which had been dried up for months for want of rain, were gurgling to their hearts' content and the crops which they produced that year were the best in all the land.'

'What happened to the little boy?'

'He became a hero, and, if the truth must be told, a bit too big for his boots.'

'And the giant?'

'Blubberguts? When he got home, Blubberguts was scolded by his wife for getting so wet. He had to gargle for a bit because of his sore throat. The neighbouring ogres couldn't make him out at all, because he had been pretty beastly before and now he went about being nice to people. The thing is he had learned that it really wasn't much cop making life so jolly unpleasant for everybody.'

'So the story had a happy ending after all. I didn't think it would somehow.'

'And you're disappointed?'

'Well, a bit.'

'All stories should have happy endings. When you get to my age you'll want them to. The trouble with you, young feller, is you're too blooming modern. Now keep quiet because I'm going to read my book.'

'But London's here, and we're all getting out.'

'By golly, you're right, blast it.'

A few years after this I was visited in the monastery at Downside by my two friends, Eric and Godfrey. Eric was directing a play in Bristol, and Godfrey had arranged to take in the Bath Festival on a round which combined business with pleasure. Together they drove over from wherever they were lunching and I received them in the stoneshed where I was at work on a statue. Theatre talk is not quite like any other, and I enjoyed it. I had not seen either of them since we had met at the Garrick.

'You remember who was there that day?' said Godfrey. 'Well, he died a few months ago. Fifty something but he was wearing himself out, so nobody was surprised.'

'His will surprised people though,' said Eric, 'because he left everything to some obscure sort of charity and not a penny to his family.'

'That learned them,' commented Godfrey. 'But I can't altogether blame him, because they are all about as quarrelsome as he was and are stinking rich, anyway. One of them described the will to me as "darling Humphrey's last piece of characteristic malice".'

'What was the charity?' I asked.

'Something to do with providing holidays for slum children.'

95

ISN'T THIS WHERE WE CAME IN?

She threw her head back and screamed. Not once or twice, but scream after scream: helpless, abandoned, shocking. When witnessing this sort of thing one thinks that it could not have happened in a worse place. This was what I thought when the woman screamed in the Underground lift at South Kensington Station.

The gates had only just closed when she began, and the two minutes of unhurried ascent seemed an age. In the lift was the cross-section of metropolitan life which would be found in any Underground station during the lunch hour. There we all were, with our blank expressions, our parcels, our newspapers. Each of us in our glass box, separate and insulated. Then had come the first shriek, and it was as if a shiver of electricity went through the crowd. We were still in our glass boxes but no longer so comfortably insulated. The current did not rouse concern and sympathy. It was a resentful, almost a hostile, reaction. Embarrassment tinged with vexation. The instinct was to turn away and look at the theatre posters on the side walls which showed smiling stars of revue and cinema. These popular favourites, looking so gay, and swinging their legs with such careless grace, were separated by a thousand miles from our tension in the lift. People might be laughing and singing outside, upstairs in the open, but nobody had a right to look on so confidently down here in the lift while a woman was losing control of a sorrow or a sanity.

She was facing me as we stood packed together waiting for the spasm to subside, and I could see, each time her mouth opened, the grey metal filling on her teeth.

By the time the lift clicked to a stop and the doors rolled back, the paroxysm had spent itself and the woman was sobbing. She sobbed convulsively into a handkerchief which she twisted round her fingers and which was beginning to tear. It was no relief to her to cry. In fact it seemed to be requiring further effort, her shoulders hauling up gouts of weeping. Her hat was crooked, and everything about her looked crushed and crumpled.

I wondered if she had looked so forlorn before she had broken down, and whether, if she had not broken down, I would have noticed her. Probably she was just as ordinary and dull as the rest of us in the lift. Our faces might have been composite faces, coming together to make the anonymous type-face seen on television commercials and forgotten instantly: the face over the sink, the face smiling at the toothbrush, the face aghast at the dirty floor. I took a look at the faces in the lift, and saw what I might have been expected to see: each of us was wearing his own mask. I wondered if behind every mask there was an emotion which was trying to break out. All that had happened was that one mask had cracked. Perhaps it was touch and go that a lot of others had not. Mine for instance.

'You'll be all right, dear,' a voice was saying as we poured out of the lift towards the sun and sanity of South Kensington. 'What you want now is a quiet sit down. Take my arm, dear, and we'll find a little place where we can get a nice strong cup of tea.' The speaker was one of the many millions of old ladies who are never noticed but who are always there. They emerge out of the background on occasions like these, and then disappear again. Their vague profiles, indeterminate clothes, undefined accents, their whole dim neutral anonymous selves render them invisible in lifts as elsewhere, but all the time they are only waiting to come forward with their supporting arms and cups of tea. If the tribe ever dies out it will be the end of civilisation.

Standing for a moment at the entrance of the station and watching the traffic, I felt curiously confused as to where reality left off and unreality began. I have found this before on occasions when the normal flow is interrupted: you look for something solid to stand on while you are getting your breath back. Nothing could be more normal than the man selling papers from an upturned box, the woman behind her bank of flowers on the step, the girl staring at gold sandals in a shop window. But what was going on inside, and was each of them engaged in hiding a real self which would turn out to be highly disturbing if we knew what it was? The rush of feet along the pavement, the glare of the sun and the blue of the sky, the moving line of cars, buses, vans: what lay behind? Everything round me seemed to be saying 'you don't know what we really are, and we can't afford to give away our secret; look what happens when the defences are down . . . like that woman just now in the lift . . . let yourself go for a minute, and where are you? Safer not to pry into what's beneath the surface . . . better to put up screens . . . screens are everywhere; the whole world is made of them . . . screen it, then, screen it, and don't give yourself away.'

A taxi clumsily changing gear as it came round the bend echoed the 'screen it' of my fancy, and for a split second I was able to see under the surface of things: sound, sight, smell, and touch seemed to lift like the lid of a box. Or rather it was like seeing through the lid of the box at what lay inside, and to discover that the contents bore a relation to the design on the lid. The lid could give no more than a faint indication of what was inside. What lay inside was the important part, and if one did not get that part right one would miss the point of the design on the lid.

In these rare moments of ice-clear perception, moments which carry a false promise of permanence, all sorts of dead theories stand up and become alive. Plato's disdain for familiar objects, for instance, had always seemed to me a piece of arrogant boasting. What right had Plato got to say that reality could not be perceived by the senses and that the everyday furniture of our lives was unreal? An unproven speculation, making no difference to the way we exist. Real or unreal, the things which we bump against and fit into the pattern of our lives are those with which we have to concern ourselves. So why bother? But now, standing at the entrance of South Kensington Station and watching these familiar things in their familiar setting, I suddenly found myself seeing them in a new way and as if for the first time. Just for that minute the idea was academic no longer: it might not be particularly helpful in the practical way, but at least Plato was saying something and not dreaming up a proposition which nobody could refute. Already I felt the vision slipping from me − this perspective which I thought would be with me for good − so in an effort to hold on to a formula which would bring me back to the subject later on, I shut my eyes and told myself firmly that the world consists of immaterial forms of which sensible things are no more than the unreal manifestation, and that qualities have no existence in their own right but merely inhere in what is beyond perception. Then I opened my eyes, looked at the London scene, and wondered why on earth the theory had seemed so important a moment ago. It meant nothing at all to me now, and Plato was a bore.

'Are you in a hurry? Because if you are not, I would like to have a word with you. I was standing next to you in that lift — not that this is a valid excuse for imposing myself on you.'

The speaker was a man, grave and elderly. He was tall, thin, pale, clean shaven, good-looking though not strikingly so, and dressed in a serious way. I told him I was in no hurry.

'How very kind,' he said, speaking with evident relief. 'Now if you don't mind we must find somewhere where we can sit. It's not that I mean to keep you for long, but simply that if I don't sit down soon I'll drop in my tracks. You see, if that woman hadn't screamed when she did, I would have. I was about to and was prevented by what I saw. It somehow released a tension. You would think it would have the opposite effect, wouldn't you?'

As the question did not need an answer I was silent. We walked towards the Cromwell Road. I was able to have a good look at the man who was walking at my side and who was too much occupied with his thoughts to notice the study I was making of him. 'He is getting his story ready,' I told myself, 'so I hope it is worth hearing.' I wanted to assure myself that I was not about to listen to the rambling confidences of a lunatic. What I saw told me that while he might be on edge, my companion was certainly not raving. In fact he looked the picture of sanity and sobriety; not even, as I would have preferred, an eccentric. I put him down as a barrister or surgeon. I felt that I ought to know who he was and that I had seen him before. Had I heard him lecture? Was his face familiar from the picture papers? It was no good, I could not place him. I decided that having stood next to him in the lift I had subconsciously taken in his features which I was now, after the woman's screams had expelled them from my memory, recalling. It did not seem a very probable explanation but it would do until I found out who he was. I was a little surprised that he had not given me his name; I was determined not to give him mine.

'Where are you taking me?' he asked. 'Not, I hope, to a church.'

I told him I was making for a bench which I remembered to be within hailing distance of the Victoria and Albert Museum. I thought that if anything was likely to have a steadying effect it would be the sight of the Victoria and Albert Museum. No nonsense about that building. Stability, the Establishment, security. I thought too, though I did not say so, that the open air and the passing of cars along the smooth road would be soothing to his nerves.

'I suppose most people,' he began as we came in sight of the bench, which was fortunately unoccupied, 'would be more inclined to scream after a distressing event of that sort rather than before. You may wonder why in my case it was the other way about.'

I said something about having no great desire to scream at any time.

'Ah, you are of course a priest, and therefore must be used to scenes.'

That he knew me to be a priest and not any other sort of clergyman caused me no surprise. He could hardly have mistaken my shabby hat. What surprised me was that he should associate the priesthood with scenes. It evidently suggested to his mind a life of varied excitement, priests living cheek by jowl with the more flamboyant types of mortal sin.

'Now,' I said. We sat down. It was very hot.

'I mustn't bore you,' said the man at my side, folding his fine slender hands over the handle of his rolled-up umbrella and leaning forward so that his chin touched the knuckles, 'but I'm afraid I shall have to go back a bit. To the time when I was four.'

I tried not to show my dismay. Again I wondered if a man who on ten minutes' acquaintance took his listener back to when he was four could be perfectly sane. But once more I felt forced, after a quick glance, to discard the suspicion.

'It appears that for three days just before my fifth birthday I was lost. All the usual attempts were made to get on my track, but I must have given the police the slip because when I got home I arrived by myself. This took place in India. Do you know India?'

I shook my head. 'You mean you simply walked in from the street,' I said, 'and announced that you were back?'

'No, it was not like that. You see I did not know I had been away.'

'A sort of Mary Rose?'

'Well, not exactly. Mary Rose, if I remember, turned up quite calmly after a complete blank. In my case I was discovered on the veranda at two in the morning shaking with fear and bleeding at the nose. It was a week before I could even speak, and for a time they thought I wouldn't get my speech back at all. When finally I was able to talk I couldn't give any sort of account of where I had been or of what had happened to me. It wasn't that I was too frightened to tell or couldn't bear to think of it; it was simply that I didn't know. I still don't know. All I knew was that I had been playing in the garden one minute — before tea in broad daylight — and was lying on my back the next minute in the middle of the night on the veranda. Where the three days in between should have been there was nothing. Or rather there was this: sheer fear. Stark fear, unrelated to anything except itself.'

'No inhibitions afterwards? No shrinking from the sight of a snake or the sound of a flute or anything like that?'

'Nothing apart from that one unknown dread. I was treated for shock, of course, but I wasn't an easy subject to treat. It was before they had become so expert at digging down into the subconscious. The only conclusion to be arrived at was that I was not deliberately hiding anything.'

'Nightmares?'

'Yes, there were nightmares. At least, as often happens in these cases I believe, there was one nightmare. It recurred at intervals. But a recurring nightmare throws no light on a problem when the person does not know what the nightmare has been about. I could no more give an account of the nightmare than I could of what had happened during the three days.'

'But you connected the two?'

'Oh yes, I connected the two. But look here, you mustn't think I grew up in a state of continuous dread or that I was having this nightmare once a week. As time went on the panic grew less, and though I was constantly being reminded of it I did not spend all day brooding. At the age of nine I was brought back to England for my schooling, and everyone assumed that I was a perfectly normal person without a worry in the world. Both at prep school and public school

101

I was the average boy, and I doubt if my parents even told the authorities about it.'

The names of the schools were familiar to me but since I had no knowledge of either I did not press for further information. But from what was told me next it seems that the period when he was at his public school marked a stage in his story.

'Towards the end of my last term — I was to leave at Christmas and go abroad until the beginning of the university year — I got laid out playing rugger. It was during a match against an army team, and was therefore rather rougher than the ordinary inter-school game. Anyway two of our own players were knocked out in the first half, and I got a kick on the head in the second which produced a mild concussion. Now the school doctor had left the ground a few minutes before so as to attend to the two youths which had been injured — they were being taken down to the school on stretchers — which left me without the ordinary medical attention. I say *ordinary* medical attention, because when I came to my senses again I found myself being examined by an unfamiliar doctor. He had evidently walked on from the touchline. You know the sort of thing that happens: there's a silence, and both teams stand round looking awkward; someone says "man hurt", and a housemaster comes on to the field with a doctor. (For all I knew the doctor may have been a parent.) Then after a bit people clap, and the game goes on. Anyway when I recovered consciousness after those two or three stunned minutes I knew something which had been hidden from me for more than thirteen years. I knew at last what had frightened me that time in India.'

At this point in the story I suppose I began to show interest. But if the quiet man at my side noticed my answering spark he made no effort to blow it into flame. In a dry matter-of-fact voice he went on talking.

'Don't mistake me here. It was not that the happenings of the three missing days were made known to me. As to events and the surrounding scene I was as much in the dark as ever. But I knew now that what had frightened me was a face. It was a face, too, which the recurring nightmare was all about. If you have ever been concussed you will remember how quickly, on coming round, impressions follow one another in the mind. The first, the instantaneous, reaction was

102

one of relief. There was I, don't you see, lying flat on my back in the muddy rugger field with my nose pouring blood all over my chin. The relief at knowing the solution was no more than a flash. It was followed by a renewed fear. Whatever pain I felt from the kick on the head was forgotten in the anguish of the new fear.'

'I don't quite understand. You mean a new violence was added to the old fear? I should have thought that knowing what the trouble was would make the thing less terrifying. If the explanation was simply a face, I don't see how any face could be so horrible as to make you more afraid than you were before. But perhaps I have misunderstood you.'

'It was not the expression on the face that upset me. Strictly speaking it was not even the face itself. You see, when I came round, having made my discovery, the first person I saw was the strange doctor bending over me. And it was his face.'

I looked steadily at my companion on the bench in Cromwell Road. He was a little whiter perhaps, but he had not moved an inch. He was not in any way dramatising the story. A passing Londoner would have thought him to be weighing up the architectural merits of the Victoria and Albert Museum. Struck by his composure, I felt that there would be no danger of upsetting him if I asked for further information.

'But could you be *sure*? After all you were hardly more than a baby at the time of the first experience, and there had been a long time in between. Might you not easily have been jolted by your knock on the head into making a false identification? Or again wouldn't it have been possible that before you fully returned to consciousness you saw the doctor's face, and then, after perhaps another instant's lapse, looked up and saw it a second time? These things happen so fast. I am sure a brain specialist would tell you that two glimpses of the same face in the space of a second might well appear to the concussed man as being separated by years. And in your confused state it would in any case be difficult to recognise a face seen long ago and in a completely different setting.'

'Your doubts are understandable of course. But I can assure you absolutely that I knew him at once. And what was more I knew that *he* knew. That was why he was there — so as to be present while I was making my discovery. He wanted to confirm my knowledge immediately afterwards by showing me the proof. It was the cruelty as much as the disclosure itself which caused the dread. I already dreaded the next move. I could not believe that this man, whoever he was, would let it go at that.'

'Who in fact was he?' I asked. 'Enquiries would presumably be made about a stray doctor who walked on to a private field and started taking over a concussion case. Did they tell you who he was?'

'That was the curious thing about it. Apparently he had not been invited by anyone, and nobody saw him leave the ground. The school authorities asked a few questions, but when it became clear that I was not seriously injured there seemed no point in pursuing the enquiries. So for the time being he faded out of the picture.'

'For the time being? You mean you have seen him since?'

'Certainly I have seen him since. A number of times. That is in fact the difficulty, because it is the fear of seeing him again that is now the main dread. The fear which I felt the first time in India when I was four — even the fear which I felt the second time when I was eighteen — was nothing to the fear which I came to feel as these reappearances were repeated. So you will understand that when I saw him this afternoon —'

'You have seen him *today*?' I almost barked the question at him. I was less calm now than he. 'You have seen him here in London?'

'In that lift. That is why I so very nearly screamed.'

For a while there was silence between us. What he had told me seemed all the more fantastic because of the prosaic surroundings to our conversation. The policeman at the crossing, the passers-by with their parcels, the hot pavement and tarry road, the graceful white line curving in the sky where a plane was altering course: these were things of every day. Which was the more real: the every-day or the kind of thing I was listening to? I sought for the understanding of Plato's idea but it had escaped me.

'Surely there wasn't anyone so very terrifying in that lift?' I said, deciding to forget about the inward and keep the investigation strictly to the outward, 'I am sure I would have noticed an exceptional face in that crowd. I did happen to have a look round as a matter of fact, and they all seemed to be as ordinary a collection of people as you would get anywhere. But of course I wasn't seeing the person, whichever one he was, as you were seeing him. I gather that this chap wouldn't be frightening to anyone except to yourself?'

'Exactly. People would not notice him. I have seen him mixing in every sort of company and always he's taken for granted. I've come across him in a ballroom, I've watched him eat. I've felt him brush up against me in the street. He's not an apparition: he's solid enough. Not in the least sinister to other people, he holds a particular terror for me and for me alone. Years ago I used to move about a good bit in connexion with my job, and I always hoped that this would shake him off. But he would turn up suddenly in Paris, in the Middle East, in Canada, and each time there would be the same look of recognition, the look of *reminding,* which would send me into a lather of fear. I gave up the job I was doing, and took up law. For no reason that I could put my finger on I didn't see him for some years. I thought he had given up, I even began to wonder whether I had not imagined the whole thing from the concussion stage onwards – which is of course your own opinion at this moment – but then, when I was a barrister with the beginnings of a practice in London, the whole wretched business began again. As prosecuting counsel on one occasion I was faced with my man in the witness box. It was so unexpected, and the prospect of questioning him in the open court was so unnerving, that I collapsed and had to be carried out.'

'Had you not spoken to him before this time?'

'Never. I had heard him speak, but never to me.'

'So you were afraid of what he might say?'

'Well, let me put it this way. It was the knowledge that he knew more about me than I knew myself which was the most disturbing factor. It was knowing that he still had something up his sleeve. All I had to go upon, remember, was the fact that this man stood for the fear. I still did not know what the fear related to.'

'Don't you think that if you could once bring your fear into the open,' I said, trying to be helpful, 'you would rob it of its terror? At present you have only got hold of half of it. Get hold of the other half. Find out what the whole thing is about, and it won't be so bad. Whatever this man's secret is, granted that there *is* a man and that there *is* a secret, it can hardly be worse than the ignorance and suspense which you are having to live with at present. Next time he turns up, challenge him to show you the content of those missing three days.'

There was a long pause before he replied, and I wondered if he was trying to make up his mind to accept my suggestion. But it was not that.

'For some time now,' he said in a low even voice, 'I have been coming to the same conclusion. I hoped you would say what you have just said. That is why I got hold of you in the Underground station. Thank you very much. I must now think out the approach. Forgive me for being such a nuisance.'

I expected him to get up, shake hands, and walk away. Instead he sat motionless, his chin resting on the handle of his umbrella. He looked straight ahead, unblinking and unseeing. I got the impression that there was still a decision to be made, and that it was costing him a good deal to arrive at it. I reflected that if I had been bored at the beginning of the recitation I was certainly not bored now. Indeed I was glad that the interview was not over: I might as well hear all that was to be heard. For some minutes I watched the passing stream of traffic, and then thought it time to do a little prompting.

'Don't talk about it if you would rather not,' I said, 'but this man of yours must be getting on. Allowing that he was a quite young doctor when you were four it makes him a good age now.'

'That's one of the funny things about it: he's always the same age. The first time I saw him I did not of course connect him with any particular age. Children don't think of how old people are. There are grown-ups and not grown-ups. My man was grown up. I knew this when I was able to look back on it during the concussion incident. So by the time I first saw him *consciously* he was a man in early middle age. Late forties I would judge, fifty at the oldest. He's been that age ever since. It has given me an uncanny feeling catching up. I'm now, don't you see, considerably older.'

'Doctors and actors stay young,' I said rather facetiously, 'it is only schoolmasters and priests who reveal the ravages of age.'

'Forgive me; I have left out a lot. I should have told you he was a doctor only that once on the rugger field. He assumes any calling he likes. He can belong to any nationality he chooses. On some occasions I could swear he didn't know a word of English, but at that moment, when confronting me, he knew my whole history. He takes great

106

care every time that I should be aware of this. Only once have I doubted this knowledge on his part, and that was today when I saw him in the lift.'

'Well, there you are,' I said, triumphant, 'surely you must now feel that the whole affair is either a delusion from the start or else just a series of coincidences.'

'I wish I could feel that, but I'm afraid I can't. *My* side of the experience is quite beyond doubt, and to come up against a doubt on his side of it only pushes the solution farther away. My only hope, as you yourself said a moment ago, is to get hold of the key to those three missing days. The coincidence suggestion makes it worse, not better. The point I must get clear is whether it is more painful to know or not to know the secret of those three days. This you have been very kindly helping me to do. I have now decided that the only way to peace of mind is to go ahead and find out what happened in India more than half a century ago. The only trouble now is this: what if I cannot get the secret out of him? *That's* the point now, don't you see? What if he can't tell?'

I admired the man's courage. He was prepared to face the fear in each of its aspects, and pin it down until he had killed it. He was clearly no neurotic. If his fear obsessed him, it did not take away his spirit. I did not understand the fear — how could I? — but at least it was real. It was real to him anyway.

'It seems to me,' I said, 'that you are not afraid of the man so much as of his secret.'

'Not even that. I am more afraid of the idea than of either the person or the mystery. It's the idea I have of the person that needs exorcising, and the idea of the original incident. All the way through it is the idea. If I could only open out the idea and look at it as though it were a photograph in an album, I could face whatever it revealed. Horror can't be more than an adjunct. Horror isn't something in its own right.'

Whether because of this last observation of whether because of his use of the word 'idea' (Plato's word), my mind went back to what I had been thinking earlier in the afternoon. The inward was showing itself to be infinitely more significant and real than the outward. Life was shaped more by ideas than by things. Sitting next to me on a bench in South Kensington was a man whose experience was hideously real. It was hideous and real because it was an idea. Whether it was factual or not was not for me to judge. The manifestations of the idea, the mutations on the theme, were only so many accidentals; they were not real in the way that the idea was real. Contingencies might recur under different forms but they would still be only contingencies. The circumstances of some people's lives reappear again and again in cycles, but circumstances are only the setting and furniture of life: they are not life itself. I wondered if I could convey this to the man next to me. I wondered if it would be any good if I did. I decided to try.

'The only constant,' I began pompously, 'is the immaterial form, the underlying reality. It is called by different names: being, essence, *logos,* idea. You are right when you say that in what you have told me it is the idea which is haunting you. The man is only the vehicle. The secret itself, which gives him his hold over you, is no more than a conductor. The reality of the fear is inside you. When we talk about an idea being a "conception" we mean that the inward takes shape, comes to birth, lives in a way which can be sensed. The outward can come to mean more than the inward which gave it life. The evidence, the hard fact, can be misleading. It can carry too much weight, and make the idea seem irrelevant and unimportant. So far as I can judge from your story you have allowed the outward appearances to dominate, and since the appearances are calculated to cause alarm you have allowed the alarm to assume too great a proportion in your life. Goodness knows I am not charging you with weakness. and I am sure I would be just as much dominated by fear if I were in your place; I am only saying again that the only way to exorcise the fear is to change your idea of the whole thing.'

'Well one thing at a time. You mean first of all that once an idea becomes a concrete reality it loses, if it is an alarming idea, its mystery?'

'It does not lose its power to hurt, but at least it is not pressing on the spot where it can hurt most.'

'I see. So the first thing is to call its bluff. What happens next?'

'What happens next is that your idea of the whole situation is changed. Up till now you have been obsessed by the facts as much as by the fear. When you have forced the issue you will be able to meet both fact and fear on your own terms.'

'And their significance will dwindle accordingly. Wait a minute while I think this out. You see there are practical difficulties.

'I am in no hurry,' I told him. 'After all this talk of ideas I shall enjoy looking at solid buildings, massive rubber tyres, monumental pillar-boxes.'

Trees rustled their leaves behind us. In front of us women clopped by with prams and dogs. Why did one have to probe? What did underlying principles matter? Were there not enough surface realities to keep one going over a lifetime? Yet by posing such questions one was back again at ideas.

'You may have noticed,' I said (by which I meant that I had noticed) 'how everything tends to repeat itself, moving on any number of wheels which impinge on one another but which never break the overall cycle as set in the created order. All the time we are carried according to a planned rhythm, and every now and again we catch an echo of what we have heard before. Round and round we go, seeing likenesses everywhere and hearing refrains which are unexpected but familiar. There is a sort of divine symbolism about everything we experience, about everything we come across.'

'I grant you that,' he said in the casual dry tone which he had used all along, 'but it does not help in this case as much as it ought to. The rhythm or cycle or whatever you like to call it has been interrupted, and I don't see how it can be restored.'

'If there's anything in your story at all,' I said cheerfully, 'of course it can be restored. The next time the mystery man comes along you will have your opportunity handed to you. That will be the moment to jump on to the wheel and pin him down to an explanation.'

'I wonder,' he said, turning to me. His look was so frank that I felt I had known him for years. 'Because that is exactly what I have been trying to do. But if the man fails to recognise me I'm worse off than I was before. This afternoon in the lift it dawned upon me that I might be too late. I now have a new fear: the fear that I may never know.'

'I see,' I said, cursing myself for not seeing sooner.

'You were close to me in the lift, remember, and looking straight

109

at me. I have lost my chance, haven't I? You don't know, do you? You don't even recognise me, do you?'

He threw his head back and began to scream. Each time his mouth opened I could see the grey metal filling on his teeth. A crowd formed but there was not much concern for the central figure. It was curiosity which made people stop and stare. But there was one rather gratifying reaction: somebody offered an arm for support and suggested a cup of tea near by. As I walked away I told myself that this was about the worst place for such a thing to happen. The traffic murmured, the prams rolled on, the trees rustled, the Victoria and Albert Museum did not budge.

THE NOONDAY GUN

During the days immediately preceding the Second World War, days of dazzling sunshine which belied the cloud, I was staying at Looe in Cornwall. A friend of mine was ill in the little dolls'-house nursing-home up on the hill to the west of the harbour, and I was to be on hand in case I was wanted. A twofold anxiety: the imminence of war and the crisis of a sickness.

The Catholic church at Looe was served from Polperro, and the parish priest, a certain Father Lyons, who normally came over on Sundays and once or twice during the week, had handed over to me the key together with the handful of faithful who came whenever there was Mass.

My duties as a supply were not heavy. I was expected to open the doors between seven and half past in the mornings and lock them again each night at nine. Because of the double emergency, the general one as much as the personal one, I planned to spend a night in vigil before the altar.

After the last sickroom visit of the day I walked down from the nursing home to the church in the town. I did not look forward to spending the next twelve hours in church. Whatever self-righteousness I felt was smothered by reluctance. It was getting dark and people were beginning to switch on lights. On account of the heat, or perhaps on account of a holiday mood which faraway politics could not disturb, windows and doors were left open. I could hear people laughing. There was the after-supper clatter of plates. Someone was singing the hit tune of the moment. In the street a boy, his head bent low in concentration, was bouncing a tennis ball on the pavement.

I remembered the other, or as it was called, the Great War. The twisted bodies hanging slack over hurdles of barbed wire. Trenches, mud, sandbags, howitzers, posters, war-trophies, hand-grenades made into money-boxes, crutches and bright blue suits, bandages, casualty lists, medals, *Chu Chin Chow*. Would all that begin again? It seemed impossible that Looe would be touched by it.

It was not yet nine so I left the road and went down to the water's edge where I watched the warm sea, impervious in this sheltered shore, heaving and then subsiding with only the faintest sound among the rocks. Gentle amateurish little waves smacked the sides of the fishing-boats moored at anchor in the bay. The sand, wet under my feet, made sucking noises and smelled of seaweed and salt. How could there possibly be war?

By the time I came back towards the church it was almost nine, and people were waiting to hear the news. The washing-up was over, and the boy had stopped bouncing his tennis ball. As I let myself into the small grey church I could hear from a dozen ground-floor rooms the voice of the announcer telling Britain what was happening beyond the boundaries of Looe. 'Sudetan minority . . . Mr Chamberlain's last-minute appeal . . . Polish Corridor . . . Herr Hitler's reply . . . Italy's reaction . . . France's determination . . . Danzig.' It sounded as unreal as the names announced in a ballroom scene on the stage. From where I stood I could see families sitting round their wireless sets trying to take it all in. They had listened to so many emergency bulletins that their minds were ceasing to register. Their faces showed concern: concern was the expression which they brought to each broadcast. What they were feeling was what I was feeling: the summer evening with its gnats and its hint of a cool breeze. Like me they were feeling personal things, not international ones.

While getting ready for my watch at the altar rails I reflected on the way in which the mind can take in things up to a certain point and then no more. Saturation point: an unlovely term. The public concern which had lasted for days, my own private anxiety which had lasted for days: these things left a numbness which refused further response. The emotions were there, but suspended. They were only waiting to come back and hurt. For the present everything must feel remote and unreal. Like automatons the listeners in the houses all along the street outside were turning to their radios; like an automaton I here in the dark church was turning to my spiritual securities. Nothing felt real. Nothing *could* feel real. We had all had enough.

More than thirty years before, when I was a small boy in Alexandria at the age of six, I used to wait every day for the gun to go off which announced the hour of noon. During the season of Ramadan the gun was timed for six in the evening. I made a habit of watching the clock in the hall and then going upstairs to the night nursery a few minutes before the time. A window in the night nursery looked out upon a bay at the far end of which was the fort from where the gun was fired. The fort was over a mile away, but seen over the water it looked closer. What I waited for each day was not strictly the boom of the shot nor the puff of white smoke, but the interval between the two. I liked counting the seconds for the sound to catch up with the smoke.

Kneeling in the church at Looe I remembered the midday ritual. I felt that the war had already been declared, that my friend in the nursing-home on the hill was already dead. The gun had gone off but we still had to wait. We were seeing puffs of smoke, unreal and miles away. The sound of the shot would reach us later, unmistakably clear across the water.

I need not give an account of my vigil. For most of the time I was more or less awake but this is as much as I can claim. Between four and five in the morning I must have gone to sleep properly, because shortly before six I woke up to find myself lying propped against the confessional. A rattle at the door told me what had woken me, and I got up feeling stiff and stupid. If this was to be a sick call it would not find me at my best.

After some fumbling with the lock, my fingers being without circulation, I got the door open. The air felt fresh after the staleness inside, and there was not a sound in the streets of Looe. Two people were standing on the strip of path leading to the church porch, both of them young and looking so wide awake as to put me to shame. Hikers clearly. Both were in shorts, and I thought at first, in the uncertain light and with my eyes still full of sleep, that both were boys. But it was a girl's voice which spoke.

'I'm afraid we have disturbed you, Father, but any chance of a Mass about now?'

'Not for another hour and three-quarters. I'm sorry.'

'Seven-thirty. That's what it says on the board. We came last night to see, Ted and I. But somehow I thought there might be a six o'clock

Mass as well, so I told my friend here we'd take our chance. Didn't I, Ted?'

'That's right,' said Ted. He looked as if he would like to go back to bed. I felt sorry for Ted. I knew he did not stand a chance.

'My friend isn't a Catholic,' the girl explained. 'Not yet, that is, but he will be. He's taking instructions from the parish priest at home. With any luck he'll be received before Christmas. In the diocese where we come from they are very particular. But oh my, it does take an age. Still, better be on the safe side I suppose. Ted is ready to wait, aren't you, Ted?'

'That's right.' Ted was used to waiting.

I suggested their going off and coming back again for Mass at seven-thirty. This was no good because they were keeping to a timetable, and were due somewhere along the coast later in the day. To emphasise the point Ted slapped two road maps together. The untalkative can convey a good deal in unconscious action.

'Of course if you are fasting,' I said to the girl, 'you could receive Holy Communion at any time. Now if you like.'

She jumped at the idea, and the three of us came into the unlit church. I watched them unhitch their bulky rucksacks which they leaned against the base of the font. I heard her whisper that *of course* it was not irreverent to bring camping things into church, and that he was not to be silly. I went off to get the altar ready.

So as to give the girl time to prepare for Holy Communion I lingered over the light switches, the candles, and finding the key and stole. I could see the young man self-consciously studying the five remaining pamphlets in the Catholic Truth Society box at the back of the row of benches. A coin was dropped through the slot, and I wondered which of the five he had chosen. Then he squeaked in his new studded and oiled hiking boots to where the girl was kneeling, and rather awkwardly knelt down beside her.

After fumbling about in the unfamiliar sacristy I came to the sanctuary wearing a lace cotta and a stole which was so stiff and broad that it knocked against my knees as I walked. Before going up to the altar I went over to where the girl was kneeling and said, 'Please pray for a special intention: for someone who is dying.' Rather to my relief, because I did not want to be looked at, she kept her eyes

114

tightly closed while I was making my request. She nodded her head two or three times, but said nothing. It struck me as being a satisfactory way of dealing with such a request.

Her thanksgiving, for one who must have been in a hurry to get on with her hike, was a long one. Ted meanwhile, whatever he felt about keeping to the timetable, sat back and read his pamphlet. He was used to taking second place in the partnership and did not seem to mind. Then, as I was reciting the office of Prime to myself, I heard a great sigh, and the girl, with a no-nonsense sign of the cross, stood up. Sweeping up her young man she led the way out. I was clearly expected to follow, so for a few minutes we talked at the end of the path by the spiked iron gate leading into the street. It was full daylight now and there were people walking about.

The two young hikers worked their shoulders under their heavy packs – he tightening the straps for her – while I stood by, marvelling that they should so exactly conform to the cover of the guidebook and equipment catalogue. The khaki shorts, the sleeveless sweaters over open-neck shirts, the rolled up waterproof, the tin mug suspended from the heavy but trim and efficient kit. Also matching the coloured cover were the fresh complexions and sunburned limbs. His legs were brown and firm, hers pink and less firm. Both wore thick white rollover socks which all hikers wear whether in Greenland or the tropics. They gripped their sticks: metal-spiked staffs which meant business. I guessed that they had been bought in the same shop and at the same time. 'Ted, let's have those with the silver badge near the handle. Even if the price is a bit steep. We'll cut notches for each of the mountains we go up. O.K.? That's what they do in the Alps.' The spiritual home of these two was not Looe but the Matterhorn.

'No, I don't think it will rain, Father,' she was saying, 'and even if it does we don't mind. "Dare all, like all" is my motto. Besides, rough weather will give us an appetite. Won't it, Ted?'

'That's right.'

What was Ted? A student in some provincial university? A junior master in a secondary school? Perhaps he and she worked in the same post-office or telephone-exchange.

'You see, Father, it's all according. If there's a war, then Ted will have to be in it. If he's in the War to End All Wars, then he won't be a Catholic by Christmas. And if he's not a Catholic, we don't get married. Not until he is. I'm not marrying a heretic for anything, oh no. It's a shame this Hitler with his big ideas. A proper shame, it is really.'

Her plump pink face changed so quickly to dismay that one wanted to change it back again. Just by turning a knob. Jolly or solemn she was plain, but when jolly it did not matter her being plain. Ted meanwhile was digging his spiked stick into the grass at the side of the path. A lot of little eloquent pockmarks. I thought of these two setting out on their married life together. I saw them choosing the suite of furniture ('Ted, I don't like this hire-purchase lark: money down or not at all, O.K.?' 'That's right, love, money down.'), reading their *Universe* every Friday, going to Mass with their *Sunday Missals* and *Simple Prayer Books,* bringing a tribe of plump pink children into the world.

'But we mustn't keep you, Father. Priests are always busy. Thanks for the trouble. I'll pray for that intention of yours, and I hope that friend of yours will get better. Ted will pray too. Won't you, Ted?'

'Me? Yes, sure. That's right.'

My mind still ran on, and I hardly realised that they were saying goodbye. I was thinking how they would go to Walsingham because they could not afford Lourdes, how they would cheerfully sacrifice holidays so as to get the children taught by the nuns, how they would kneel in the rain to get the Bishop's blessing.

'Oh dear,' she was saying as she held out her hand, 'let's hope there won't be war after all. Trouble all round, that's what.' Then, perhaps because of my hangdog appearance (I had not shaved, and my habit was dusty from the bare boards on which I had by mistake slept) and perhaps because of the intention for which she had promised to pray, she made a remark in a different key. 'They tell us to pray, and go on praying. That's right, and I'm not denying it. But praying isn't the whole story, is it? Not the whole story, Father. It's paying the price, that's what. *Someone* has to pay. Oh well.'

Coming from someone else, from someone less genuine, the observation about the costliness of God's service would have sounded either trite or sententious. To me it was neither banal nor pious. I made no reply. Apart from making use of Ted's favourite phrase there was nothing much I could say.

As I closed the door and kicked the mat back into position, I could hear those square-toed alpine boots scraping their way, in step, along the pavement which led to the green hills overlooking the river valley of Looe. I picked up the breviary and started the office of Terce. Next day my friend in the nursing-home died. Two days later Great Britain was at war with Hitler's Germany.

Four years – as we used to be told in block capitals half way through the silent film while appropriate music was played at an upright piano half hidden by ferns and palms – elapse. Instead of Cornwall the scene is Somerset. The atmosphere is no longer sharp with anticipation but flat with four years of war. The time is a November afternoon.

I was kneeling in the nave of Downside Abbey waiting for my half-hour of mental prayer to end. I could hear a party of visitors moving from chapel to chapel and little bursts of whispering. From the clop of their heels on the cement floor of the aisle I judged them to be women. I did not look up, and I sensed rather than heard the approach of one of them. She had detached herself from the rest and had tiptoed to within a few feet of me. I could not go on for ever pretending that I had not noticed, so I opened my eyes and got up. I recognised her at once.

She was in the uniform of a WAAF, and had grown a little plumper. She was just as pink and jolly-looking as before. Uncomplicated, friendly, unspoiled by world or war. She looked at me with frank eyes in which there was no hint of recognition. There was no reason why she should know me again, but I was surprised. Why I did not remind her of our meeting four years earlier I do not know. Too often I shrink from taking the initiative and regret it afterwards. In an impersonal voice I asked if I could help her. The usual formula.

'May I have a Mass said, Father, for a friend? It would be nice to have it said in the Abbey here if possible. No hurry; any day will do.'

She went on talking but I was not listening. I was remembering details which I had not consciously taken in at the time. The comb marks in Ted's hair, the gilt pencil clipped to a pocket of his shorts, the way his thumb fripped the tops of the road-maps as though he were about to cut a pack of cards, the ring on this third finger.

I looked to see if there was a ring on her third finger. There was not. Her chubby hands were blue and chilblained, and round like her legs. I felt sure that her friends in the WAAF made jokes about her legs. She was talking now about how she had been to Buckfast, and how glad she was of the chance to see Downside. As she rambled on I began to listen again.

'I want to see all the abbeys eventually. All the ones that are *used*, I mean, like this one is. Not the old ones, like Bath and that, because there's no monks in them. It's wonderful coming to a place like here, Father, and to know everything's going on just as in the Middle Ages. These friends of mine are just thrilled. I knew they would be, so I told them they'd have to come next time we got a day off. A day's *leave* I should say. All non-R.C. but very friendly. I think one of them may become a Catholic. I'm lending her books about it.'

'Is this friend of yours a Catholic? The one you are having a Mass for?'

'He was received a year ago. But I should have explained. He's dead.' Though her expression changed, it was only for a fraction of a second. In a perfectly matter-of-fact voice she went on quite naturally to tell me how they had planned to get married this year, how he had liked the Irish priest who had given him his instructions in North Africa, and how lucky it was that the same Irish priest had been able to give him the last sacraments. 'This chaplain, Father Casey, writes to me even now. He was very struck by Ted, how good he was and that. Edward, that's the name for the Mass, Father. And you'll be saying it, will you?'

'I'll say it tomorrow.'

I wished I could meet Father Casey. I am sure he had helped Ted through the profession of faith and his examination of conscience. I could imagine Ted, at intervals during the instructions, nodding his head and saying 'That's right'. I doubted if he did much challenging. No mental gymnastics for Father Casey.

I know I should have told her, before saying goodbye, that I knew Ted and was sorry. But this is a true story, and I must simply state that I did not.

'Well, I must take my little lot back to the depot or there'll be trouble. I won't ask them to meet you because they said they were shy and didn't want to. Priests scare some people. They don't me.'

'Goodbye,' I said shaking hands. Perhaps because I knew Father Casey would do all this so much better than I was doing it, and perhaps also because I hoped she would recognise the reference, I added, 'Some have to pay the price, don't they?'

'Pay the price? Don't they just — but it's worth it.'

Evidently she did not catch the echo. An echo which is four years old is not easy to catch. Also she had been addressing me four years ago on a subject which I was not likely to forget. But now, this time, I was addressing her. I was referring to something which she would not forget.

'Come along girls, all aboard. And if we are shot for desertion it will be my fault for talking so long to this priest.'

As I watched her shepherding the blue-grey figures towards the door I had the curious fancy that this afternoon's visit was not a random haphazard thing which happened to have about it an element of coincidence. It was the sound of the shot catching up with the puff of smoke.

AMERICA

WATERS OF THE MISSISSIPPI DEEP AND STRONG

In August 1959, a warm summer in the United States, I gave a retreat to the Carmelites at Jackson, Mississippi. I thought I had reached the stage in preaching and giving retreats when nothing new could happen. Shipwreck apart, my apostolic journeys had compared not unfavourably with St Paul's for lively incident. If I could not claim to have been lowered over a city wall in a basket, I doubt if St Paul was ever interrupted in a sermon by an elderly lady who threw down her hearing apparatus, battery and all, on the floor and jumped on it. Would, again, the Apostle be able to match with an experience of his own the occasion when, without warning and when I had got well under way, an electric fan which could have served as the propeller of an ocean-going liner spun into action with such force as not only to roar my words into immediate silence but also to sweep my pages of notes to the opposite wall where they remained, flat and still as though glued, until the pressure of the gale was, as suddenly, released?

Other misadventures have, in the exercise of my functions as a lecturer and retreat-giver, admitted me to the unexpected. Engaged to speak about St Benedict, I learned from the amplifiers in the auditorium that those assembled would now learn from me the principles governing modern art. On another occasion I was introduced from the platform as Father Zundel, the celebrated author of *The Splendour of the Liturgy*. At a Poor Clare convent a cat sprang first upon my lap during a discourse and thence to my shoulder where it sat, purring and uninhibited, until the end.

In a hall at Denver I enjoyed the privilege of being listened to by upwards of six hundred nuns, assembled from different communities, all of whom were eating ices off the ends of sticks. The distribution of ices, efficiently conducted row after row by a member of the home team, took place during the earlier phases of my address so from the elevated position which I occupied on the platform I was able to lay bets with myself as to which religious order would finish first.

Then, to go back in time and place, there were the retreats in England during the War. A two-day retreat which I was giving to dockers in Bristol opened and closed to the wail of sirens. The first discourse was delivered in a cellar which was so imperfectly ventilated that for the second we moved upstairs. By the end of the retreat we were so hardened to the hazards of war as to sit through air-raids without bothering to shut a window. During the Battle of Britain I was giving a retreat at Salperton in Gloucestershire, and between the conferences, delivered against distant gunfire which sounded unconvincing, the retreatants would lie out in the sun in deckchairs watching the puffs of white smoke high up against the blue of the sky. Tiny glints of silver, trails of black, specks of gold.

The Carmel at Jackson represents to me a retreat different from all others. For one thing it is the only place I can remember where I have felt hot, hotter than I would normally choose to be. The temperature during the eight days that I was there varied between a little below and quite a few degrees above a hundred Fahrenheit. I had come from Memphis, Tennessee, where it was not cold either.

I left Memphis by air in the glow of a sunset to remember. Unforgetable is the burnished metal wing under its wash of red light, each little button furnace-hot until the sun finally sank and the plane became pewter. Two young people, friends of the Carmelites, were at the airport to meet me. I judged them to be engaged, or soon to be. By now it was dark so as they drove me across flat country to the convent I had little chance of seeing what the South was like. The dry crackle of insects, the dust, the peculiar smell which is composed of withered plants, blistered woodwork, dried manure: it reminded me of Egypt. The car was an open one, and though it travelled fast the air came hot against one's face.

'You'll love it here, Father,' said the girl.

'It's a great place,' said the boy.

'You'll find it quiet at the convent, Father,' said the girl.

'They sure leave you alone,' said the boy.

The Mother Prioress had given them the key to the chaplain's rooms — it was long past the time when the nuns could be up — so the two young people showed me where everything was, had some coca-cola and cookies which had been left out, said goodbye and went away. The crickets were chirping, the grasshoppers were whisking and frisking their zigzag courses, and somewhere a bird (a corncrake perhaps?) was keeping up a harsh monotonous cry. The chaplain was away so I had that part of the building to myself.

'I hope you have brought plenty of things to do,' Mother Prioress said next morning when I went to the grille to pay my respects and learn my duties, 'because apart from the three discourses a day and a few confessions you will have time on your hands. It is very quiet here.'

I assured her I had got work to do and was glad to have the time for it. She need not give me another thought; I was never bored.

'This is not a very Catholic part Father, so you won't find people dropping in to see you as they do in many other states.'

I would not be lonely, I told her, and was pretty unsociable anyway.

In Carmelite convents you do not see the nuns face to face. In addition to the grille there is a curtain or a shutter. You very soon get used to this, and it seems the most natural thing in the world not to be conscious of the age, appearance, or expression of the person to whom you are talking.

Hardly had I got back to the sitting-room from the interview with Mother Prioress when I saw a line of small children, walking in crocodile two deep, pass the window. It turned out to be the lowest grade in a school near by whose teacher was a Catholic and who thought it might be a good idea if I gave them a little talk about the Bible. So they all trooped in and sat on the floor, fifteen to twenty of them, and we had great fun. There were coloured children as well as white, and I have seldom met a group I have liked more. Then they all knelt down, Catholics, Baptists, Orthodox and Jews, and chanted in a high monotone, 'Please give us your blessing, Father,' and I felt like a bishop.

In the afternoon a young man came from the local broadcasting and television station. He wanted me to appear that evening in an open forum programme. It was to take place at seven, and he added 'live'. It was this that spared me, because at that hour I was down to give the evening discourse to the community.

'Isn't that too bad,' he said, dismissing the idea with a flick, 'but here's what we'll do instead. Forget about the TV panel, and just do a ten-minute to quarter-of-an-hour broadcast. I'll pick you up so you can be back way before seven. We'll have your talk at six, right?'

I said it was impossible. I was sorry to make difficulties, but it could not be done.

'How come?' he said, and then, obligingly, 'Why not?'

I explained that the rules of the English Benedictines forbad the publication or broadcast of any script not bearing the seal of official censorship.

'Where's the problem?' he asked, raising his shoulders and showing me the palms of his hands. 'We tape you at the studio, the tapes are dropped off at the Chancery, the Bishop has some guy listen to what you've said, the tapes come back to us with the official seal, and you go on the air at six o'clock. Okay?'

'If the Chancery takes the responsibility, okay.'

I telephoned to the Chancery and arranged to present my credentials in half an hour's time. The young man from the studio drove me first to the Chancery and then, the permissions obtained, to the glass cage from which I made my first broadcast to the United States of America.

Next morning, after a night spent largely in thinking of the clever things I might have said in my broadcast, I received a message from Mother Prioress asking me to come to the grille when the morning conference was over. I gave my talk at ten and was in the parlour at ten-thirty.

'The Sister Infirmarian thinks you need a tonic, Father. You look tired after yesterday. We are sending a little fruit drink to refresh you; it will come through the turn in a few minutes. You must drink it, Father, and don't forget you are meant to find rest and quiet while you are here. We must see that you are not disturbed by visitors.'

I thanked her, confirmed my statement of yesterday that I was one of nature's recluses and never met people if I could avoid it, and sat down to await whatever might be sent through the turn. The turn is a revolving cupboard on which trays, books, objects of piety and so on come from the enclosure to the outside world and by which they go back again. I heard a woody knocking and rattle, a whispered *Laus Deo semper,* and round came a tall tumbler on a triangle of tissue napkin.

A currant or raspberry cordial holds scarcely more attraction for me than soup. But at least this dark drink looked cold, and it did not fizz. Ice bobbed and tinkled against the inside of the glass, drops formed on the outside and rolled down the frosted surface into the tissue napkin. With the thermometer standing at an easy hundred in the shade the sight was a pleasing one. I drank almost the whole lot in one go, and only when I put the glass down with the dull klonk of ice at the bottom of it did I realise I had been drinking port.

Contemplating this phenomenon with the glass in my hand ('Where else but at a Carmelite convent would I get iced port? . . . I didn't know one *could* ice port . . . what is the quickest remedy for iced port?') I heard a car drive up to the door. Through the window I saw a young man in light trousers and a sweat-shirt, who, it turned out, was coming to see me. He looked as though he had enjoyed every moment of his life up till now and was likely to enjoy the rest of it without a reflex thought.

'Hi, Father, remember Mike and Carol May? The kids who fetched you from the airport? I'm a friend of theirs, Cy Becker.' We shook hands vigorously. 'They said to tell you too bad they couldn't come, but they got their morning all loused up. So they had me come instead, okay?'

'How very civil of them – and of you too. Please thank them from me.'

'Now I figure we have more than an hour before you eat, so I just have to do what Carol May said and take you for a ride.'

'I haven't ridden for years.'

'Not horseback riding: riding in a car.'

'That would be nice. I'd better change. Wait here.'

'Sure. You don't have to change, but if it makes you feel any better go right ahead. I'll wait.'

The religious habit is not worn out of doors in America, and the

126

excuse to change clothes gave me a chance to put my head under a tap of cold water as I had seen people do in films. It did no good. In a few minutes we were roaring down the drive in an open sports car. I asked Cy where he was taking me.

'All over I guess. And when you've seen what the town is like we'll take a look at the zoo.'

'The zoo?'

'Sure. Don't you have zoos in England? You know — animals. Animals like this . . .' He lifted both hands off the steering wheel and gave a passable imitation of a monkey. 'And birds, like this . . .' He flapped his arms, and this time it was an eagle. 'Yeah, our zoo here in Jackson is quite something.'

So after a quick tour of the city we drove under the burning sun to Jackson Zoo. I have never visited a zoo where there was less shade. Jackson Zoo remains in my memory as a shimmering glare in which tawny beasts move restlessly this way and that smelling of hot fur and port. My companion proved a mine of information on the subject of animal life, and though I did not want to listen, being fully occupied with my own thoughts, I was prompted into giving my closest attention by a favourite phrase of his, 'let me tell you something.'

'Guess we've seen most all of them now, just about. Any others you'd like to take a look at?'

'Polar bears. And then home.'

Possessed of engaging high spirits, Cy would have been just the man for the desert island. I left most of the conversation to him. He was all for taking me out riding again that afternoon but I told him I intended, skipping lunch, to lie down until the next discourse at three, and then perhaps to lie down again.

'Sure. I'll drop by tomorrow to see how you're making out, and maybe bring Mike and Carol May.'

I told him this would be swell, and as we turned in at the convent drive I saw a car drawn up in front of the door. Seeing our approach a troubled-looking priest stepped out holding a wristwatch against his ear. Cy dropped me, said goodbye, and roared round the bend into the highway. My heart in my boots I faced the priest.

'Father van Zeller? I'm Father Sterke, the Bishop's secretary. If

127

we hurry I can take you over to see the Bishop now and bring you back after.'

'Tell me the worst, Father. It must be that broadcast. Put away the handcuffs, Father; I'll come quietly.'

'It's not that at all. He's invited you to lunch. But we'll have to be quick if we're going to make it.'

'Then let me pop in and tell the nuns I won't be lunching here.'

'I already have.'

'There's one thing I must do if you can wait a minute. I must put my head under a cold tap.' A pint of cold port was something which called for constant attention. I thought it would take too long to explain this.

'Sure, go right ahead.'

On the way to the Bishop's house Father Sterke, as Cy had done before him, pointed out landmarks of interest. He also spoke about the War. He was referring to the American Civil War. We passed a thing which I had never thought to see, either in America or any-where else, and which moved me profoundly: a gang of prisoners with chains on their ankles working on a railway line under a warder carrying a rifle. I remembered as a child marvelling at Charlie Chaplin's performance in the role of prisoner, and here in 1959 were half a dozen hapless men of the deep South wearing the same shackles and dressed in the same costume of black-and-white broadly striped cotton. Alluding to it in answer to my questioning as a barbarous survival, Father Sterke took the cheerful view that at least I need not fear a similar fate in consequence of my broadcast.

If sherry was served before the meal we fortunately arrived too late for it. Nor, I was relieved to find, were the Bishop's guests expected to drink anything stronger during the meal than tomato juice. In the ordinary way I tend to react adversely towards prelates, generals, heads of departments, and impressive people generally. I warmed instinctively towards Bishop Giraud. But I was, after the events of the morning, dumb. If the Bishop should ever chance to read these pages he will see added grounds for what he must have taken on that occasion to be my natural dullness.

With ten minutes to go before my three o'clock discourse to the nuns, Father Sterke put me down at the convent door. It left me just time to change into the monastic habit, put my head under a cold tap, and walk on as the clock was striking.

The day was still young. After speaking for half an hour in the chapel I came back to the outer world wtih only one idea in my head: to lie down and forget. Waiting for me was a reporter from a local newspaper who brought with him the press photographer accredited to the journal for which he worked.

'What we had in mind, Father, was a question-and-answer interview with a few pictures showing the convent chapel and maybe you in one or two characteristic attitudes.'

'I have no characteristic attitudes.'

'Say, what *about* that? There's one for a start off. Why don't I get that down? It will do fine as an opening.'

It was no good protesting. They led me across the yellow burnt-up lawn and took photographs of me standing next to the marble bust of Father Lord S.J., who had been largely responsible for founding the convent.

'Jesuit and Benedictine,' murmured the reporter into his notebook, 'divided in method, united in aim. That okay, Father? Has to be something which catches the eye if you understand?'

'You chaps stick at nothing do you?'

'Boy, that's another one. We'll fit that gag in some place, right? Now, Father, do you have some thought you'd like to communicate -- some meaningful message, maybe, or comment on contemporary thinking which we could incorporate in this article? Something, say, on patterns of teenage behaviour . . . The Vatican as a trend-setter . . . the Catholic image in Europe. Something of that nature? Just anything will do, you know, so we can write it up in the office. We like to leave the door wide open. Take your time, Father, it's up to you.'

'Well,' I said in my pompous English way, 'the visitor to the South sees many reminders of the past: blackened chimney-stacks bearing witness to a war of long ago, gaols still retaining ancient penal usages, cotton-fields unchanged since they were picked by the hard dry hands of slaves. To me it is a matter of interest that so much remains the same when what I would have thought were some of the better elements of your history have been discarded.'

'Like what?'
'Prohibition.'

Next morning when she met me at the parlour grille after the discourse, the first thing Mother Prioress said was how much better I looked as a result of the tonic she had sent through to me.

'But Mother Prioress,' I scolded, 'you might have disgraced me. You did say, remember, that it was only some sort of fruit juice.'

'Well, what's wrong with that? Port comes from the grape, doesn't it? We were really worried about you, Father, so I had one of the sisters call a Catholic friend in town and ask him what would put blood into the veins of a tired man. People in Jackson are very kind. He came by within minutes and left a bottle for us. The ice was our idea.'

If the hospitality of nuns is ever in question, I can confidently provide an answer.

BROTHER JUDE

I am writing this in St John's Hospital, Springfield, Illinois. Though not allowed letters I may spend an hour's manipulative therapy each evening at the typewriter. So I am catching up on my diary. There is a notice on the door saying that there must be no visitors, and most of the day, thanks to repeated sedatives, I spend in sleep. I mean to make use of this evening's period of wakefulness, and tomorrow's as well if I do not have time to get it all down now, by recording a visit I received yesterday.

'Good morning, Brother Jude . . . good morning, Brother Jude . . . good morning, Brother Jude.' It might have been said three times or thirty. It reminded me of the way in which radioed messages opened: headquarters telephoning to the police car. Except that I seemed to be hearing it from inside a glass tank of water or through several thicknesses of cotton wool. Like the policeman in the car I felt the necessity of giving to the message my whole attention, so, after a struggle with the combined weight of sleep and conscience, I managed to wake myself up.

'Oh, good *morning,* Brother Jude.' And there the radio stopped. The message had got through.

What I saw in front of me at the end of my bed was a nun carrying an armful of flowers and smiling with great sweetness. Yes, you are right: I thought I beheld a vision. It took me a moment or two to get the vision into focus, because the nun seemed to go up and down and her outline seemed to come in waves, but eventually my eyes found the range and I was presented with an ordinary straightforward vision of a steadied-down standing nun with flowers.

'I'm surely glad you've waked,' said the nun, 'because I just couldn't go right back without you even saying Hi.'

'Hi,' I said.

'Maybe I'm kind of a surprise to you, Brother Jude, coming in

like this with "No visitors" on the door and all, and you not knowing me to speak to, but I figured if I didn't look in and you heard
about it afterwards from the Clancys you'd be mad at me. Isn't that
right?'

'Mad,' I said; 'who are the Clancys?'

'*Say* . . . who are the Clancys? You *must* be sick. Well now, I was
visiting with the Clancys and the kids Sunday, and Kate said, "Next
time you go down town, Sister, why don't you stop by at St John's
and say Hello to Brother Jude, the Redemptorist who's in there
convalescing after surgery? He'd be real pleased. And give him the
best from all of us." So that's just what I've done. And these flowers
are for you, Brother Jude.'

'But I'm not Brother Jude. I'm sorry, Sister, but I'm not a Redemptorist either. My name is Hubert van Zeller, and I am a
Benedictine.'

'You're kidding. You just *have* to be Brother Jude. Look, these
flowers are for you, and they have got your name on the card: "To
Brother Jude". The Clancys know you're Brother Jude. They'd feel
bad about you if I called them dinner-time and said you were not
Brother Jude.'

By this time the last vestige of my drugged sleep had left me. I
looked squarely at my visitor — the vision idea had faded the moment
she opened her mouth — and saw there one of the nicest-looking
nuns I have ever seen. Even for America, where nice-looking nuns
abound, she held high place. Fresh complexion, frank eyes, mouth
set in a continuous gleaming beam of good nature: the kind of face,
though of course without the make-up, which you see on every
poster in America whether advertising beer, air travel, intimate
articles of clothing, sparking plugs or beauty cream. Though feeling
the benefit of this pleasant, and almost more than human, radiation,
I experienced at the same time one of those convictions which are
beyond gainsaying: I knew that I was in the presence of the stupidest
woman in Christendom.

'Sister, let's put it this way. You came to do a kind act. You have
accomplished your purpose. Now you can return to Mr and Mrs
Clancy, give them back their beautiful flowers, and greet them with
my kind regards. The kind and grateful regards not of a Redemptorist

132

brother but of a monk from England. Then everybody is happy, even Brother Jude because he has known nothing about it all along, so he is happy in his ignorance.'

'From England. Wait till I tell the kids I teach in school. They're crazy about Princess Anne and Prince Charles. England. That's *right*. I read a book one time by an English Redemptorist. It adds up fine now; we're getting some place.'

Conscious that any place we were getting to must be the wrong one and that whatever was added up could only bring the sum to an answer which was not in the book, I headed her away from Brother Jude and the Clancys by trying to steer the conversation round to herself.

'So you teach, Sister. That must be very rewarding. I don't recognise the habit. Is your order devoted exclusively to teaching? You have not told me your name yet, you know.'

'Sure I've told you my name, over and over. Sister Felicity, and I'm real happy to meet you. I belong to the Transfiguration Sisters. I've said that before too, but could be you were asleep.'

'Could be,' I said, Anglo-American co-operation in mind. So I had missed something, had I? I had come in at the 'good morning, Brother Jude' and had imagined this to be the beginning.

'Say, do you have a vase anywhere around? It kills me seeing these flowers die.' Vase was rendered 'vaise'.

'It's most kind of you, Sister, but really I'm not entitled to them.'

'Wait a minute, Brother, the Clancys meant them for you, didn't they? You've just been saying that it's the intention that counts.'

'It may count as far as the donor's merit is concerned, but it doesn't necessarily count as far as the recipient's responsibility is concerned. You must be careful not to get this doctrine wrong. There's a common error here. For instance it was a disciple of Gautama Buddha who held that so long as you wished something on someone you satisfied the obligation, and it was the same as giving the person that thing. His theory, later repudiated incidentally, was that if a stranger came to you asking for a horse —' I was well away now in my best lecturing manner, very pompous — 'it did just as much good if you drew six pictures of horses on six peices of parchment and threw them out of the window. You may have the noblest intention in the world but you also have to think of what is likely to reach the recipient — the right recipient.'

'But I don't draw too well. And I never could draw horses.'

Sensing quite rightly that we had reached another deadlock, Sister Felicity took the flowers from their tissue paper, put them in the basin, and turned on the cold tap. Then she opened the shiny black briefcase which she had been carrying, and took out a pair of fishnet gloves and a small book. The gloves surprised me a little but they went with her trim black habit and ironed veil. The book she opened at the title-page, handing it to me with a gilt ball-point pen. I observed how deft she was in her movements: much more nimble than in her mental processes. If I had wondered earlier that she had been given the work of teaching, I could see her now in the classroom where she would be distributing exercise books, flicking ball-point pens, snapping a drawer here and a cashbox for the missions there, regulating the thermostat and the air-conditioning, switching the fluorescent neon lighting on and off. I would suppose she got as good results as her sisters in the classroom next door with all those degrees.

'I would like for you to write something in this before I go. It's for little Brendan Clancy who's being confirmed a week Tuesday, on the feast. He'd sure like that; it would be a real privilege. Could be he'll flunk the diocesan examiner's test — it's oral and there's a slight personality problem involved — but if I have anything to do with it Brendan'll make it. Just put your name right here.'

I hesitated. The longer I hesitated the more uncomfortable I became. Could I persuade myself that I was Brother Jude after all? No, but at least I could persuade myself that the doctrine of the good intention could here be applied in its widest possible sense. Grasping the ball-point firmly, I wrote: 'I sure hope you won't flunk . . . forget about that personality conflict . . . here's wishing you all the best, from your old friend, Brother Jude.' Ought it to have been 'flunk *out*' or was the bare 'flunk' correct? Anyway it was too late now.

'That's swell. I appreciate it. And I'll have Pat come visit with you just as soon as that notice about no visitors is off the door.'

'Pat Clancy this would be?'

'Why *no*, Brother Jude, what can have gotten into you? Can't you remember *any* of your friends? Pat Dunn. Maybe I've tired you, so I'd better go. Well, the news I'll take back is that you look fine, just fine, and that your surgery —'

'Surgery? Oh yes, operation. Well, I haven't had a surgery. Not that it signifies, so dismiss if from your mind. Just tell the Clancys and the Dunns and everybody "Hi" from me. And thank you so very much for coming. Most kind.'

'You're welcome.' She was gone. I sank back on my pillows and closed my eyes. It was no good. Brother Jude was far too wide awake.

HOLD IT, COWBOY

After an accident to my ear I have not been able to balance properly. As this sometimes so affects my walking that I swing from side to side, my legs even crossing under me like a pair of scissors, I try not to assume that people who sway and hold on to the wall, who plunge suddenly sideways and collapse in a heap, have had too much to drink. Yesterday my laudable resolve received its first setback.

I had steered a zigzag course across the tarmac from the terminal building to the plane, stumbled uncertainly up the steps of the gangway under the eyes − it might almost be said under the eyelashes − of two trim and shining air-hostesses, and finally tumbled into the farthest of three empty seats. The worst part of the journey was over; at the Chicago end I would not have so far to walk. I put my hat and breviary on the seat next to mine and a file of papers on the one next to that. It is always my hope that I shall have time on the plane to prepare my next retreat; so, as the opening conference was due in six hours, I wanted to make sure of being able to go over my notes. It never works. Invariably someone leans over from the other side of the aisle and says 'Pardon me, Father, guess I got a problem', and my preaching material goes unlooked at.

Yesterday was no exception. Hardly had I arranged my face to express expectation of a friend who would be sitting next to me but who was cutting it rather fine, when a troubled looking man walked by and then turned back. I might have guessed. He was a long bony man of about thirty with a brown face and hairy hands. He wore a pale wide-brimmed stetson tilted back on his head, and his trousers were tucked into his boots.

'Mind if I sit here?' he said, with his thumb outstretched as though he were asking for a lift.

'Please do,' and I removed my belongings.

'Makes me feel better being next to a priest,' he said by way of apology, 'because when the plane crashes I got a better chance.'

I took this to be the kind of joke which people make when they want to start up a conversation with a Roman collar, but when I looked at him I saw that the man was serious. I saw too, as he dropped into the seat next to me, that he was unsteady. Here, I told myself firmly, was someone else who had injured his ear, and I hoped to goodness we would not be comparing symptoms from the time we took off till we landed at O'Hare Airport, Chicago. My companion clarified the position by saying quite simply: 'I'm drunk.'

If a man tells you he has been promoted in his job, you say 'I'm glad'. If a man tells you he has caught a cold, you say 'I'm sorry'. Not knowing what you say when a man tells you he is drunk, I said nothing.

'But you go right ahead, working or praying or whatever you figured to do,' he said as he leaned back and closed his eyes, 'it's just I'd have you know the way I am.' I thanked him and in a few minutes we were off the runway and in the air. I studied my notes.

When the notices about seat-belts and not smoking faded from their rectangles, my neighbour rose very carefully to his feet and took from a side pocket a pint flask, unopened, of Hiram Walker whisky, which he asked me to look after for a few moments while he went to the back of the plane. 'I'd be glad to, of course,' I said. 'I appreciate that,' he said, attempting a little bow — which missed. The politeness of Americans, young and old, never fails to impress me. I wondered how many drunken strangers in England would bother about bowing and appreciating.

In a minute he was back with two of those little cardboard cups which they provide on planes and which taste of candles. Not until he had settled into his seat, fastening the belt as close as it would go, did he flick down the tray in front of him and ask for his bottle back.

'You take it straight?' he asked, lifting out the cork.

'Not just now, thank you,' I said. He looked disappointed.

'Too bad. Maybe later.' Then he loosened his tie and undid the collar of his shirt. This is a thing I have noticed before in the American male when he addresses himself to the serious business of drinking. Where an Englishman's tie and collar may slip their moorings after a bit, an American's are unfastened as a preparation. Like a

137

schoolmaster wiping the blackboard before setting up the exercise of the day, or like the bedouin letting the folds of his garment flow free before a long day's ride across the desert, the American makes sure, by attending to the initial stages, that things will be more comfortable later on.

'Guess you must think I'm acting pretty dumb, Father, working it out this way. Right?' He drank from the little cream-coloured cup in two great gulps, and from the face he made he seemed to be disliking it. Of course, yes, it had tasted of candles. 'Don't get me wrong, Father,' he went on, 'I'm not a drinking man. Oh, sure, maybe once in a while at a party I'll get kind of sponged up, but me, I'm like I said – I'm not a drinking man.'

'I see,' I said, 'sponged up.'

'Quite a figure of speech isn't it? I just thought it up, and it surely fits. But like I said, I wouldn't drink if I could get where I wanted any way else. And if I did, I wouldn't use this kind of sauce. O brother, do I hate the taste of whisky! And this is *good* whisky at that. Try it, Father. O.K., O.K., I won't press you. Listen, I'll tell you. I'm a cowboy, see, from Montana. You know Montana? Never been there? Well, I work with cows. Cows and horses. *Way* out back. Well, I get this phone-call saying Ma's sick, so what do I do but come right along.'

'Highly commendable,' I said, getting interested.

'How's that again? Oh yeah, sure, commendable. Ma's sick – right? Real sick, in Chicago. "Poor Ma's mighty sick," I tells the boss, and he says, "Sure, Carl, you go see Ma . . . you go see Ma because that's where you belong right now: longside of Ma." So, Father, I come straight to the airport, and what do I do? I head for the bar and I buy me one martini, two martini – maybe four, maybe five. And, like I said, I'm not a guy who drinks.'

'Yo mean you drank because you were worried about your mother. I think it is a mistake to drink in this way, mind you, but I can understand the need you felt for support. You must be a very devoted son.'

'Hell, no, Father, I'm not all that devoted. Nor is Ma all that devoted to me. I haven't seen her in years. We're not too close, my folks and me. But, like the boss said, I belong in Chicago until we

138

know one way or other. It sure isn't because of what may happen to Ma that I've been taking slugs of liquor; it's because of what may happen to *me*.' Before I had time to say 'How come?', though I doubt if I could ever have said it convincingly, he bent his big shoulders in my direction and whispered with a sincerity and humility which I found touching: 'I'm scared, Father, that's what. I'm so darned scared of flying that I just got to get so I don't feel any more. Back at the gate, before we boarded, the guys in those fancy uniforms with the peaked caps like a five-star general wouldn't let me through at first. Guess they thought, "Here's this cowpuncher from the desert been swallowing the fire; we don't want him to hurrah the plane." Me, I thought I'd gotten the whole trip fouled up, and likely have to turn back. But know what? I told this guy, the top one with the radio in his ear, that Ma was awful sick in Chicago, and boy, wouldn't she be mad if I missed out. Well, it sure worked. Real nice guy, he was. Both of them real nice guys.'

'Very civil of them certainly,' I said. My appraisal sounded a little jejune, so I added, 'speaks well for America's humanitarian approach.' Which made it worse. He looked at me with a bleak uncomprehending, but not unfriendly, eye. I felt encouraged to go on, the explorer plunging deeper into this transatlantic forest, but along another path. 'Your mother now. How ill would you say she really is? They must know at home that you do not care for flying, so I imagine that the situation is grave if they have urged you make this long journey by plane.' There was a pause; I wondered if he had heard what I had said. He had heard; he was just sorting it out — translating.

'Who— Ma? You're right, Father, you're dead right. Ma's in no shape. She's in no shape *at* all. I'd appreciate it if you'd mention her in your prayers; in your Mass maybe.'

At once, on the introduction of this note, I felt myself stiffening. I hated myself for it, but stiffen I did. Not normally aware of any particular Englishness (being, though a Britisher by birth, part Belgian and part Dutch) I have only to be confronted with the born and bred American unselfconsciousness in matters of religion and I become ripe for type-casting. If even the idiom of the American citizen makes my own more pronounced — styling me inevitably as a Powell-Waugh-Sitwell and even Wodehouse character — his frankness, particularly where God is concerned, heightens my reserve.

'I would be glad to,' I said with a little cough. 'You were saying . . . about your mother.'

'That's right . . . Ma. Father, she's a doggorn sick gal by any count. First off it's this leaning kidney. But wait and I'll tell you. I have a letter here from my sister. Ordinarily Peg don't seem overly concerned, but you read this, Father.'

I read the letter. It left me in no doubt: Peg was concerned, and Mrs whatever-her-name-was must be far from well. Feeling a little sick myself I handed the letter back. The cowboy, with an expression of deepest disgust on his brown handsome face, was doing his best to get through the whisky. I was glad we were not first-class passengers or we would have been served the drinks which the rich were enjoying in the front half of the plane. When the beautifully eyelashed and nail-varnished young woman came round with cups of coffee, my companion said, 'Relax, honey, I'm making out fine.' She smiled. When a light luncheon was brought about an hour later I hoped he would eat it but he waved it away. Mentally comparing the insides of mother and son, I speculated upon the possible effects of raw spirit upon an empty stomach. Ought I to say something, stretch out the preventing hand?

'If it makes you feel any better, Father,' said the cowboy as though reading what was in my mind, 'go ahead and preach. Tell me I'm jackass stupid to be scared of flying . . . tell me drinking don't pay off. Sure I know that. Too bad it has to be this way. Flying just pulls me apart, I swear it. Back on the ranch I can break in a horse and think nothing of it. Wild beef don't bother me. I've never tried but I reckon I could handle a buffalo. Ever seen a buffalo get mad at something? No? Well I have, but I'd sure rather take on a buffalo than step into a plane. You just don't know what I'm suffering right now, Father, and I guess preaching wont help me any.'

I confess it made me feel strong and manly to be up there in that plane and not to suffer the least tremor of fear. Next to me was a young, healthy, rough man of the open, one who had fought with beasts at Ephesus and had overcome, and here was

140

I a crumbling ruin. Yet he was afraid and I was not.

'No, preaching won't help,' I said, 'but praying might. Have you ever thought of praying when you are afraid? I mention this because you yourself spoke about praying, in connection with your mother if you remember, so it occurs to me that you might try it and see how you get on. Whisky doesn't seem to be succeeding, so why not give prayer a twirl?' Anyway it showed I had stifled any English inhibitions and was ready to come into the open as a man of religion. It showed also that he was teaching me more than it seemed likely that I would be able to teach him. 'Incidentally are you a Catholic?'

'That's right. Though I've strung out some from the group, I guess. Raised a Catholic though, sure. Prayers? I haven't said any in years. Just wouldn't know how to begin. I'm not a good Catholic, Father, I'm telling you. Not a good one *at* all.'

'Well, look,' I said, 'what you are afraid of is that this plane will crash, that you will get hurt, that you will die, that you will have to face eternity one way or the other. Those are the things you are afraid of, aren't they?'

'Near enough.'

'So even putting it at its worst and assuming that all these things will happen between wherever we are and Chicago, the safest way through them is to put things right with God. You believe in God. Now is a good time to make an act of contrition and to leave the rest in his hands. That's prayer. That's faith. Get on with it.'

There was not much time to play about with. In twenty minutes we would be landing at O'Hare Field, Chicago (provided the horrors I had outlined were spared us), and before then there was an even chance on my cowboy lapsing into unconsciousness.

'Father, you've sure put me in quite a squeeze, but if you think it will help I'll give it a trial. Let's get this straight: I make an act of contrition — right? Then I put my life in God's hands — right? What comes next? You must help me, see, because I'm kind of out of condition. Then I pray . . . and that's faith. I sure hope I get this fear licked. Maybe I'll come back by air when I've done with Ma.'

'One thing at a time, Carl —' I was talking to him as I imagined his boss talked to him, or possibly even as Ma talked to him — 'let's get this act of contrition straight first. Shut your eyes if it helps you to concentrate, but don't go to sleep until you've made it.'

He closed his eyes, put his elbows on the tray-rest in front of him, and held his head between his hands. So as to give him more room I took away the two cardboard cups and the nearly empty bottle. He was absorbed and did not notice.

'How does it go again? I've got as far as "O my God, because thou art so good". How does it go on from there — something about "purpose of amendment"?'

'Listen carefully, Carl, and say slowly after me . . .' and we went through the words together. By the end of it I could hardly speak.

'You got yourself a convert,' he said, and then lay back and went suddenly to sleep.

Because of a traffic block in the air over what is one of the busiest airports in the world, the plane was nearly an hour late. The cowboy was able to sleep on, and I was able to say some Office as well as to revise my notes. Before we touched down I roused him. I had written out the address of the Cenacle where I am giving this retreat in case he should feel drawn to follow up what we had discussed. I put the piece of paper in his pocket together with the Hiram Walker flask. It took some time for him to wake up and focus his thoughts, and he sat on in his seat, blinking and nodding, till all the other passengers but the two of us had got off the plane. I hoisted him up eventually, and though I am not short he towered above me as we made our way, arm in arm, towards the door of the plane where the two air-hostesses were patiently waiting. One of these lively young women looked hard at me and said, 'Why, of all the things to happen . . .' In an equally shocked voice, and again looking straight at me, the other said, 'Am I surprised?'

Coming down the steps on to the flat, the cowboy found his voice and said, 'I figure it takes people different ways. Me, it doesn't trouble my head none, and I can speak the way nobody would notice I was drunk. Where I get it is in the legs —' he pronounced it 'laigs' — 'so I'm mighty obligated to you, Father, for your arm right now.' It was not an easy manoeuvre, my own laigs being what they are after last year's little accident, but we made the right gate and concourse in the end. Peg was there to meet him, so I left him with her. 'And I'm obligated to you for something else besides,' he said as we shook hands.

'My pleasure,' I said, feeling it was an occasion when the English formula should bow to the American. I looked about for the friends who were coming to meet me, and who had, like Peg, been waiting an hour for the plane to arrive.

'Hi, Dom,' said Mike, appearing suddenly at my elbow, 'good to see you.'

'Who was your chum?' asked Nancy, 'we were watching you from the observation deck. You seem to have been enjoying your trip.'

'Don't *you* start,' I answered.

ON THE HOUSE

'We have now climbed to a height of seven thousand feet above sea-level, yessir,' announced the ticket-collector with shining satisfaction. Since I was the only passenger in the long pullman carriage I felt that his 'we' gave added meaning. The process of mounting to this height in the Rockies had been a joint enterprise, something between the two of us which reflected credit. He pointed out of the window and said, with the zest of a feature article, 'See that post sticking up back apiece from the track? There's one every thousand feet up. We cross the line right here. We've made it.'

Why in comparison are we English so lacking in enthusiasm? I could imagine this American ticket-collector, pink and smelling of after-shave lotion, saying to his wife each morning as he kissed her over the flapjack and molasses: 'Know what, Ellen Sue? Sun-up right on schedule.' I could not imagine an English ticket-collector standing on the beach at Brighton and crying to his children: 'Cheers, boys and girls, the good old tide's gone and done it again.'

I was feeling elated. It was partly because of the altitude and the snow, but partly also because I had that morning preached the concluding sermon of a retreat at a convent in Cheyenne, Wyoming, and was now on my way to begin another retreat at the Trappist monastery near Aspen, Colorado. The discouragement would come later, in about ten days' time. For the present it was all elation.

'Okay, let me take care of that,' said the ticket-collector when he saw my clumsiness with the suitcase and typewriter, 'I figured you were a visitor when I saw you didn't know where to put the ticket. Well, this is Dulcedo. Quite a place. Have a nice trip.' Friendly chap. They all are. He was quite right about my being a visitor. I did not know the pitch.

The snow had been cleared from the rails, but even so I managed to fall into about two feet of it piled up at the side of the line. American trains, as everyone knows who has followed the fortunes of Wells Fargo on the screen, are higher off the ground than ours. So this was Dulcedo. Both the ticket-collector and the clerk at the Cheyenne booking office had pronounced the name Dullseedo, and from the look of the place my own church-Latin, which would come out as *dulchaido,* might smack of pedantry. Snow as a rule makes houses look clean and cosy, but today under the afternoon sun it was exposing an unwashed Dulcedo. The station looked like a pile of old denims.

The train had not yet moved off and was breathing steam. In the setting of Dulcedo it shone like a well-groomed silver dragon, germ-proof and gathering concentration for the ascent which would bring it to the next thousand-foot post. As though blowing on its wheels for the job, the great train puffed slowly at first and then more quickly until with an unexpectedly old-fashioned goodbye wail it left me to my speculations as to how the little town of Dulcedo can possibly have got its name.

I was still debating within myself, weighing up the alternatives of a young man honouring his sweetheart and an old one shedding his bitterness in a return to the kind memories of his youth, when an untidy bundle of a man shuffled past me in the direction which the train had taken. He halted a few yards beyond me, deciding evidently that it was a mug's game running after trains. Even if the snow had not got in his way he would not have run far because he was drunk. Aged between sixty and seventy, fine crop of grey hair falling to his shoulders, thick unclean beard of uncertain shade, muscular body running now to fat, high laced mountain boots, padded and quilted jacket as worn in Thibet or Korea, angry expression.

There seemed to be nobody else on the rails side of the station so I thought I would stay where I was for a while in case the man who had missed his train might also miss his step. After a minute or two of swaying, my fellow traveller shook an enormous fist at the horizon, drew with the other hand a flask of spirits from his padded bosom, and gave a roar such as must be seldom heard outside a zoo. Looking to see that there was nothing worth preserving he then hurled the pint flask at the rails with such force that a diamond shower was sprinkled over the snow.

Whether he knew I had been watching him I could not judge, but when he brushed past me on bumbling feet in the direction of the ticket office his look was not that of a brother. One eye seemed to be closed completely, the other was black with deep dislike and red-rimmed like the washer of a hot water-bottle. Lifting my typewriter and suitcase out of the snow I followed this colourful inhabitant of Dulcedo into the waiting room and ticket office. Here he dropped on to a bench, went instantly limp, closed the second eye, and presumably addressed himself to sleep. Many years ago I saw, though I was not meant to see, a dead pit-pony tipped from a monorail coal-bucket on to a heap of slag. It was just like that.

I should explain that though I enjoy travelling I do it very badly. So if I am to be met I allow a wide margin. On this occasion I had telegraphed to the Trappists asking to be met at 3.43, which seemed a likely sort of time for a train to arrive, and since this left me a clear hour and a half I decided to explore Dulcedo. It was obvious at once, even from the view presented at the station entrance, that like so many small towns in the West and Midwest there would only be Main Street to explore. Nevertheless I was elated, and when, crossing the street from the station, I heard two shots in quick succession I felt Dulcedo to be not lacking in promise.

Reflecting that nobody would want to take my typewriter and suitcase from where I had left them in the station I gave myself up to the luxury of imaginative reconstruction. Only when this attraction fails me shall I be ready for the knacker's yard. But today I had hardly got going with scenes of the gold rush when a police car, sirens rising and falling in accusation, sang past me in the snow. Had it been a sheriff and posse on horseback I would have made for the livery stable and joined in. As it was I walked on towards what I took to be the oldest part of the town. I was right, and I was rewarded, for in no time I found myself in front of an impressive red brick building which proclaimed itself the Hotel Dulcerado.

If there was a certain swagger about the name there was a certain swagger about the facade. It was a hotel with pretensions, built in about 1860 when pretensions ran high and when places like Dulcedo were in the running to be a boom town. The man who planned the Dulcerado was clearly not going to stop at putting up a station hotel however grandiose. There would have to be an opera house,

146

perhaps a casino, certainly a department store. (Others could supply church, school, and hospital.) 'Meantime,' he had said, 'leave me to provide the comforts of the east in the style of the west.' So there it was, the Dulcerado, facing on Main Street. If fronts could deceive, Dulcerado's front would deceive with the best of them but give better value than most. It presented an elevation which included cream stone cornices, arched mouldings (also picked out in cream) over the windows, muslin curtains gathered in symmetrical sweeps, and a bold line of lettering rendered in false perspective. A particular feature was the entrance, a handsome brick portico surmounted with a painted wooden balustrade. The swing door which must have replaced the mahogany and frosted-glass of long ago, stood, or rather revolved above a noble gradient of white-washed stone steps (now cleared of snow but not outdone in cleanliness), while let into the porch's side walls were stained-glass lights showing two young women in flowing draperies bearing paniers of fruit. Entwined into one young woman's hair, which cascaded luxuriantly to the waist, was a red red rose; in the hair of the other, above the ear, was pressed a much enlarged marguerite.

All this gave me pause. It was just the place for me of course, but was it just the place for a priest? If the bearded brigand at the station, the shooting, the police car and the general appearance of the citizenry were anything to go by, was it wise for one who planned to open a Trappist retreat that same evening to enter? True it was early in the day, but perhaps at Dulcedo the inhabitants began settling their differences and celebrating their triumphs at lunchtime. I did not want to be confronted on entry with a bar-counter running the length of the hotel and the rough laughter which can greet a man who has stumbled out of his element. But I was cold and I craved coffee. Though the sun shone and the air was as crisp as a water-biscuit the outside temperature stood below zero, and the hotel promised straining hot-pipes. I pushed through the revolving door.

If after viewing the exterior I was prepared for disappointment (which I always am) the interior exceeded my wildest western dreams. Since the ground-floor of the hotel consisted of one large square lobby with dining-room and kitchen leading off it at the back, and since this hall stretched up to the roof which was mostly of glass, a

147

visitor could take in the whole place with one look. Though the ground floor was spacious it was also depressive: the two galleries of rooms which flanked its three sides gave it a cramped appearance. It could look up at the glass roof but only through a well. The two ballustraded galleries suggested a library or a bank. At each of the far corners there was a staircase. No closed corridors, no lifts, no landings. Just open streets of rooms looking down upon an intimate and domestic court below.

Much of the original decoration must have gone. I looked in vain for the white wheels with knobs round the rim, the line of heavily tasselled silk ropes suspended from the arras and (like the wheels) serving no purpose whatever, the screens with their filigree tracery, and the fans shaped like tennis racquets. But if much had been swept away by the march of progress, a hefty lot remained. The chandeliers (wired now for electricity), the gilt-framed looking-glass over the marble fireplace (where incidentally a fire, an unusual sight in America, was burning), the velvet hangings and pelmets edged with little bobbles of yellow wool. At each staircase, standing on the inner newel was an inadequately draped female figure holding high a sort of icecream cornet topped with a fluted glass lamp. The faces of these marble ladies were turned towards the centre of the room, their expressions neither censorious nor amused.

I had seen it all before a hundred times (I had even written a film script round it which must have been so bad that the company to which I sent it did not think it worth returning) but it was another thing to be walking about in it while it was still alive. It was not exactly shouting its head off or popping corks, but at least it was still going – and not in the least self-consciously at that. Hitherto the Hotel Dulcerado, hundreds of it, had been presented to me visually and orally. Accordingly the absence of card-tables and tinkling piano registered at once. But today it was presenting itself to the senses of smell and touch, sense beyond the reach of the screen and paperback. The impact was immediate and gratifying. First the combined aroma of cigar, horsehair upholstery, beeswax, coffee; second the glow, especially after the cold outside, of American heating.

In our hygienic civilisation, where only antiseptic smells go

148

unchallenged, it is a joy to come upon the fullbodied smells of fifty or sixty years ago. Today you can hardly get the smell of brass-polish unless you go looking for it in a sacristy, and some of the most evocative smells which belonged to my boyhood – smells connected with oil-lamps, soot, horse-manure and cabs – would be difficult to bring back into general circulation. The fact that the smell of cigars dominated all other smells at the Dulcerado is significant and proves that it was a built in, endemic, indigenous, handed-down smell. Because certainly when I arrived nobody was smoking a cigar. There was one man who had a cigar in his mouth but he had not lit it.

In England we are coming round, very gradually, to the idea that it is more agreeable to be warm than frozen stiff. But we still feel guilty about discarding the old idea. So long as we cannot claim to be comfortably boiling, and so long as we mean to go into a glacial atmosphere any moment now, we accept in principle the warming of rooms. In America the question is not at issue: the houses are delightfully stifling from the first cold day till the last, and people take it for granted. Nothing could be more sensible. So it was with a sense of the fitting that I met the grateful blast. From my study of the literature I had not been ready for it. The literature had simply assumed it and not thought it worth mentioning, and a film would not have been able to record it anyway.

There were no bacchanalia going on. It might have been the Athenaeum. So I ordered coffee, quantities of it, to be served in the main hall and not in the dining-room which I could see from the door had been modernised, and in the meantime went for a walk along the galleries. Since nobody paid me any attention I was free to roam. I need have had no fears about a leg in an open-work stocking: what legs I saw were severely male and correctly trousered. Since the door of one of the rooms, clearly unoccupied, stood open to reveal an opposite door leading out on to a veranda I walked through it. The veranda proved to be a balcony running the length of the hotel on three sides with its own outside staircase. If you had not left yourself enough time to run down the stairs to avoid a bullet you could jump from the balcony straight on to your horse. Alternatively, though this would again take longer, you could mount to the balcony above and shoot it out from there. I was glad to note that these outdoor stairs and balconies were of wood and that the brickwork which had so much impressed me from the street was a piece of showmanship.

Back indoors again and on the lower of the two galleries I leaned on the balustrade and listened to the ghosts. They were easy to hear: the click and swish of the pool-table, the jumping melodies plucked out of the old upright piano with its fretwork panels and flamboyant fittings, the tinkle of glasses on a tray and the banging of bottles on the big bar-counter. But where was the big bar-counter? I had not seen it. Had room-service come to Dulcedo? Where were the hard-drinking cattle men, trappers, horse-traders? They cannot all have become as anachronistic as the lovely ladies in purple and green silk, those charmers with jewels in their hair and hearts of gold in their purses along with their deringers in case of emergency: slim waisted and tears of pure pity never far from long sweeping lashes. Where were the tinhorn gamblers with their thin moustaches and frilly shirt fronts, the drummers with their brown bowlers and carpet bags, the alcoholic judges and the curt but kindly doctors? I could see nobody below me in the lobby who was in any way familiar. Ghosts were elbowing one another in my head, shooting off the tops of brandy bottles from the hip, but with whom down there could I shake hands? 'I'll try the old chap with the unlit cigar,' I said to myself as I walked down the stairs to my coffee which was waiting.

In the glazed look of his eyes the man with the unlit cigar resembled the nymphs or goddesses who held aloft their *flambeaux* from the newel-posts at the stairs. But in other ways he differed from them greatly. For one thing he must have been seventy if he was a day, and for another he was properly dressed. Not for him the full lip, the rounded limb. A spare frame (except for an unexpected paunch) and an almost ascetic head, this cigar-chomping citizen was one of a million others who are perfectly true to type and yet who, even though I have lived among Americans, defeat me every time I meet them. To me he could have been either a senator whose lung condition required a high altitude or a janitor who was prolonging his luncheon hour. I did not have to open the conversation; he opened it for me. Suddenly unglazing his eyes he brought me into focus and spoke.

150

'Preaching hereabouts?'

'If you can call it that.'

'Trappists maybe? You're surely Catholic.'

'How do you know?'

'Guess it's my business to know what's going on around here.'

'Well, it seems you haven't missed much about me anyway.'

'Reckon it's fifty-fifty. You don't miss much about our outfit.'

'As a visitor I'm interested. Forgive me if I have shown too much curiosity.'

'Go right ahead. Dulcedo is all yours.'

'Thanks. I admit I am wondering where everyone is. Perhaps you can tell me something about the Hotel Dulcerado?'

'Sure, I own it.'

I was not in the least taken aback by this. Or if I was, I knew what was required of me. I got up from my chair and bowed, giving my name and saying how pleased I was to meet Mr . . .

'Field is the name. Frank Field. Brother Jerome at the Abbey knows me. Ask him about Frank Field. Say Hi to Brother Jerome from me.'

'I'll make a point of doing that, Mr Field. Hi to Brother Jerome. And in the meantime it would please me greatly if you could tell me a little about this town. I confess Dulcedo puzzles me. Your excellent hotel puzzles me too but perhaps it would be impertinent to ask about it. This Dulcedo now, it must have sprung up at about the same time as towns not far off but it seems to have lagged behind. I'm all for this myself; it's just that I am wondering why it isn't more like Laramie, Boulder, and Grand Canyon.'

'Guess it's because we in Dulcedo like to keep it this way.'

'I hoped that was the explanation. But it doesn't explain everything. After all you are on one of the old routes westwards to Utah, Salt Lake City, California, the goldfields. Also there would have been gold here too, wouldn't there? And then the railroad pushed up the mountains with its speculators, fur-traders, tourists. What I don't understand is how Dulcedo got so far and then stopped so suddenly.'

'Maybe industry ain't so important to towns as psychology. Gold? Yeah, sure there was gold. My father panned in creeks not five miles from where you're sitting. No call to move on to California: we had it right here on the doorstep. Furs too. Bears, moose, elk, deer. They can still be hunted within a few miles of here today. As a kid I used to set traps and load up. Oh sure, there was plenty going on around. That's why they built this hotel. Till then there were only saloons and dance-halls. There were some still in my day. Honky-tonk, gambling, liquor and gunplay. Not too long ago. Before the last of them was broken up there would be farewell parties. Even the horses joined in. Wooden buildings then of course, with enough brick and stone in them to stand up when the rest got burned down. I remember those farewell parties like it was yesterday. Having to lead the horses away from the flames. No cars then of course. I go back quite a way, don't I? How old would you say I am?'

'Seventy.'

'I'm eighty-six. Ever heard of Colonel Cody?'

'Of course. Buffalo Bill Cody, scout and fighter of Indians. Oddly enough I saw him a few years before he died. He was attached to some sort of circus which was appearing in London when I was six.'

'My, that surely is a link. I wasn't much older than that when I first met him; he was returning then from fighting in Nebraska, avenging General Custer's death. Makes it 1876. He used to come to our place often.'

'I thought he came from Iowa.'

'He did but he settled in Wyoming, downhill from Dulcedo and over the state-line. It doesn't matter where you're born; what matters is where you settle. You settled, preacher?'

'Hoping to be.' I liked the way he called me 'preacher'. It was better than 'reverend': it stated a function. But having no wish to discuss my plans I headed him back to what was clearly his after-luncheon subject. 'You were saying,' I reminded him, 'that the saloons and dance-halls couldn't compete, so dropped off one by one.'

'That's right. Dulcedo went respectable. I've never seen but one man shot in this room here, and he and the killer were both strangers in Dulcedo, come in from Montana some place. We served liquor then, see, and there was poker for those who wanted. But we didn't encourage gun-toters and fancy dans, nosir.'

'Now that you have got on to the subject of the hotel perhaps you won't mind my asking more about it. Do you mean you don't serve drinks here at all? When I came in an hour ago I expected to see a bar and a row of bottles occupying a prominent position. Your Hotel Dulcerado has the look which a variety theatre might have if it decided to become a court-house.'

'Sure, this is a dry house. If you'd noticed you'd have seen that Main Street is a dry street. Dulcedo is a dry town.'

'It wasn't very dry at the station when I came in. There was a drunk chap looking like a down-at-heel Ernest Hemingway waving a bottle about.'

'And he missed his train, right? That would be Mac. He talks a heap about quitting Dulcedo but he never gets around to boarding a train. Man, he couldn't pull out of this place. Mac was born and raised in Dulcedo. He says he hates a dry town but he's okay where he is and he knows it. Mac gets his liquor sent from out of town: he'll never move.'

'How did the change come about? How did the rip-roaring, pistol-packing little mountain community turn into the sober society it is today?'

'Took time. First off we got a good lawman. He cleaned things up some. Then we made things easy for homesteaders and difficult for prospectors. Then I guess we just went around talking. The bank helped a whole lot, and the mission. Then . . . you haven't seen our school? We saw that the teachers were men and women who belonged here. When Prohibition came in we were already conditioned, and though Prohibition took Dulcedo back to lawlessness and drink for a while it gave us the excuse we needed. So Prohibition here has never been lifted. People take it for granted. Those like old Mac who want to drink can buy it, but it's mostly kids and straight alcoholics who take the trouble to. There isn't a store in town that sells it over the counter. Not many cities, even in a so-called dry state like Oklahoma, of which you could say that.'

'Forgive me if I am being personal,' I said, looking at his fine senatorial face which by now was lit with the glow of the pioneer, 'but you like living in Dulcedo, don't you?'

'Sure,' he said for the second time that afternoon, 'I own it.'

I had been talking to the Last of the Barons.

153

WHEN THE CHIPS CAME TUMBLING DOWN

We were told at the terminal that all flights westward would be delayed. But the sweet smell of travel was in my nostrils and I refused to be dismayed. When we flew out from Boston's surprisingly unpretentious airport I was in high spirits. The temperature had been below zero for much of my visit to this part of the country — I had been preaching a retreat at the Trappist abbey of Spencer — but instead of reducing me to numbed incoherence it had lent wings to the material I had prepared, and I was still glowing with pleased astonishment. I was now on my way to give another Trappist retreat, and if there is one work which I enjoy more than another it is this. Vanity is a great spur, and I was exhilarated. But the main reason for my elation that morning was the permission I had received the day before to prolong my American mission for a term of three years. The grant allowed for a further extension if no obstacles were to come up in the meantime. All I had now to do was to secure a worker's permit, and I had been told that there would be no difficulty about this. The future promised well.

In the plane, where soft music was played before takeoff, I must have presented a picture of satisfaction. I beamed on any whose eye caught mine. Cold men came aboard, saw me, thawed out and said 'Hi'. Rich old enamelled women nodded at me over their orchids. Babies stared, dribbled, chuckled, held out sticky hands. I have noticed before that when one is bursting with satisfaction one becomes immediately the recipient of confidences, so it was no surprise to me on this occasion when a fellow passenger left his seat and came to sit down next to me. It was my fault, for I had purred myself into a state of comfortable reverie which was calculated to last for hours, but instead of reproaching myself for an idiot I made ready to spread sweetness and light.

'Maybe this constitutes slender grounds for an introduction,' said a cheerful voice at my side, 'but you remind me of a dead uncle.'

'Let us get this clear,' I said. 'Am I to understand that I resemble your uncle in death or as he was when alive?'

'This may surprise you,' he replied, 'but the answer is – both.'

'Ah, so the position needed clarification after all.'

'Fond as I was of my uncle, it is perhaps fortunate that he is no longer alive. Doubles can be an embarrassment to one another.'

'Oh, I don't know. Think of the fun your uncle and I could have had, filling in each other's gaps. Much more fun than twins who can't help it. Twins either complement each other's lives or else reproduce them, and this must be very dull for them both. Doubles on the other hand lead completely different lives, so it is all the more exciting when they meet. I should like to have met your uncle. Tell me about him.'

'Guess he was a happy kind of guy, and now he's dead. That's about the whole of it.'

'Well tell me about yourself then. It is so seldom I want to hear about other people, and listen to their stories, that I must make the most of it. Today I am enjoying an undeserved euphoria, so spin it out and you'll find me smiling like a Chinese philosopher.'

He spun away, giving me plenty to smile about. He was a good talker, full of wit and shrewdness, so the time in the plane went quickly. He told me he was a journalist, married, aged thirty-nine, not a Catholic, a graduate of Harvard. His daughters were being taught by nuns, and he said he would not mind if his son wanted to become a Catholic and a priest. 'Catholicism doesn't appeal to me,' he admitted, 'but I believe in the idea of vocation. I believe in everyone following his own call, regardless of what is expected of him.' He had clear-cut ideas about war, happiness, morality. I imagine he had clear-cut ideas about everything. When he asked about me I told him I hoped to stay on in America, and that this accounted for my good humour. 'Yeah, you surely look as though things are going well – too well.'

'Too well? Can they? I mean ought one to question that?'

'I remember when I came out of the army. Everything was going to be fine from then on. The war was over, my job was waiting for me, I had found a house which was dead right, and a wife who was still more dead right. But you know I have since come to realise that

155

to be all set for security and happiness is not always the best thing. I don't say this cynically. It's just that happiness doesn't work out this way. When the prospects are a hundred per cent promising a man would be wise to offer sacrifices to the gods.'

At Seattle both of us were to change planes. As we walked towards the terminal buildings — to the high screech of engines and across an acre of concrete spotted by the pale pats of trodden-in gum — I felt that here was someone who was no longer an acquaintance. He liked the things I liked, laughed at the things I laughed at, took seriously the things which were serious to me. Since we still had an hour before boarding our respective planes, we ordered coffee and sat talking.

'Having the cards dealt the way you want it isn't enough,' he said, his mind reverting to a subject which I thought he had dropped. 'I suppose it's man's most common mistake to generalise about happiness, and his next most common mistake to identify it with a place or a job or a person.'

Our table was near the counter so the girl who brought our coffee heard what we were saying. She seemed amused, and when she tore the slip of paper from the pad which hung on a chain from her belt she laughed outright. My companion looked up, smiled, and said, 'Tell us what's so funny.'

'It's his English accent I guess,' she said, indicating me with her pencil. 'You know who he reminds me of? He speaks just like —'

'Like your dead uncle,' I interrupted.

'Why my dead uncle for heaven sakes?' she laughed. She would not say of whom she had been reminded, but her laughter tinkled over our table like a crystal chandelier. I felt more and more years sliding off my back. If this goes on, I thought, I shall be remembering how it felt as a boy to laugh . . . not analysing laughter as we do when we are older, comparing it as I am doing now to quite different things. Just for a moment I did remember.

The man opposite me tipped his cup, pouring some of his coffee into the saucer.

'Why do you do that?' I asked.

'It's a libation to the gods,' he said.

A few minutes later his flight was called, and mine immediately after. Flying out from the horseshoe of mountains I congratulated myself upon having spent such an agreeable day and having maintained my mood of elation. The sun was setting as we headed towards Portland, Oregon, where I was to open the Trappist retreat that evening. I could hardly believe I had left snow-covered Massachusetts only a few hours ago and was now looking down on the States of Washington and Oregon which were basking in hot sunshine. I had skipped spring altogether, and would be landing in the equivalent of an English summer.

Among the first out of the plane I bounded down the gangway, and was met at the gate by the Abbot of Our Lady of Guadalupe who grasped my arms in welcome as though I had arrived from another planet. I felt I had.

'I have a cablegram for you,' he said, 'from England.' He handed it to me.

My mother told me once that when a telegram came for me I held it as though it were a sleeping snake. I remembered this while fingering the Western Union envelope.

The cable told me of Dom Julian Stonor's death the day before, and recalled me to Wales where I was to take his place. I knew what awaited me: days which followed one another like black leaves on the surface of a canal. I wished I had written down the name and address of the man with whom I had been travelling from Boston to Seattle: a man always likes to be proved right.

WALES

CAMBRIAN JOURNEY

On top of it all the train was twenty minutes late. I stood on the wet platform of the little Welsh station, and, unusual for me, regretted the impulse which, some seven hours earlier in the day, had propelled me into the silver mists and purple mountains which looked so attractive in the coloured handbook. I had lost my way, missed the bus back, lunched off a single banana, and was now soaked to the skin. At my side under the dripping shelter stood the station-master, and through the grey wet dusk we watched the absurd engine pompously puffing up the incline as though pretending to be scornful of the timetable, and then grind to an asthmatic halt immediately in front of us.

'Is it ever punctual?' I asked.

'Now and again, like, now and again,' said the station-master, 'but there's reason on her side today, you understand. Good reasons you might say.' One of the reasons became immediately apparent: there was a band aboard. If it was not in full, it was at least in three-quarter, blast. The metal and the woodwork of the toy train rang to the strains of rich Welsh melody.

'Snowdonia's answer,' I said, 'to the challenge of Glyndebourne.'

'The boys are serious right enough, mind, and mean no harm, look you.'

Wondering at the significance of this oblique statement I boarded the train. The corridor was swaying with men holding in square hairy hands bottles of beer, the compartments were filled to capacity with men blowing into musical instruments. There seemed to be no women passengers, but instead there were quite a few sad-eyed, saintly looking, shivering whippets. As I squeezed myself into a seat between two warm moist Welshmen I heard a whistle, and through the window I saw the station-master sliding out of my life with a knowing look. From that moment onwards until we reached our destination I seemed to be in the middle of a rather mad dream: never have I felt less in my element.

160

The 'boys' were mostly middle-aged, some were about seventy. But all of them, certainly, boyish. I like being able to place people within minutes of meeting them, but this lot defeated me. Was this a parish outing? Were they football fans, returning from a game? Dog-racers? Musicians on hire for the afternoon and now free to slake their thirst? There was probably a simple explanation, but I felt too much of a stranger to ask for it. The boys would have been ready enough to answer questions, but in the general air of geniality it did not occur to them that there were any questions to be asked. As they took me for granted, it was assumed that I so took them. In the intervals of blowing into brass the boys offered me beer and tobacco with tipsy magnificence, but there was something lacking in me because I felt more at home with the trembling whippets than with the warm revellers.

The illusion of being caught up in a dream was heightened by the outdated appearance of the boys. The thick-soled boots, the high-cut waistcoats, the soup-plate caps and generously braided bowlers: it might have been a photograph taken on August 4, 1914. The figures of the boys were squat, firm, square — as though assembled with spanners — and nearly everyone wore the thick moustache of the silent film.

'No more beer, Mr Evans, then, lad?' asked a flushed man who stood uncertainly in the doorway, and who, presiding over a crate of bottles in the corridor, was evidently acting host. 'Not giving in is it?'

'The wife doesn't like it, see, if I'm never too steady on me pins coming home like,' replied Mr Evans with a resigned but still thirsty look. 'Thank you, Mr Hughes, boy.'

Mr Hughes laughed loud at this, and the others in the compartment joined him. There was no malice in the laughter. Laughter, bursting in great gusts through the pipe-smoke, was the instant reaction to every observation. I envied the ease with which it was possible, in that company, to be a wit. Not that my fellow travellers were drunk — they were no more than what is called 'nicely thank you' — but they overflowed with a beery good humour which was probably their normal habit. That they should address one another so formally, using the prefix 'Mr', surprised me since they must have been friends of long standing. I find myself constantly surprised by the *mores* of Wales. Less unexpected was the habit of tacking on a noun to the name.

'What about you then, Mr Owen trombone, lad?' said the generous Mr Hughes bottle, slapping a very old gentleman on the chest with the back of his hand.

Mr Owen, who was wearing a hearing-aid, blinked his rheumy eyes behind steel-rimmed glasses and sadly shook his head. His trombone days must have been long since over for he had no teeth, and his lips were sucked in so that only the thinnest line of mouth appeared.

'And him with no wife, look you,' brayed another voice, 'so what's to scare him on his doorstep, eh?'

Mr Owen opened his mouth and cheerfully answered this sally, but although I was within a few feet I could make nothing of what he said. All that reached me was the sound which you hear when a surgeon pulls off his rubber gloves.

'Oh, aye,' said Mr Hughes with a tremendous gale of laughter. But he was bluffing. He had not understood a word.

Then, as if from the signal of a conductor's baton, they all tuned up, and a moment later there was music. Singers as well as instrumentalists bumped their way down the corridor to our compartment and joined in. Empty bottles rolled on the floor; those still containing beer were held between the knees. The noise was deafening. At the end of the ballad or hymn or whatever it was everyone was breathless. The noise of the train and the panting of the passengers came as a sudden anticlimax, and a whippet, supported on the lap of a man opposite me, raised its head and whined.

'A nice little meeting we had back there, then, wasn't it?' said the owner of the whippet. The remark was as much to distract his dog as to contribute to the conversation. Patted and stroked, the whippet put its head down again between its paws, and gazed, after a glance at the beer-wet floor, across the carriage at me. It was the sort of look St Perpetua would have given to a fellow Christian in a Roman nightclub.

'Aye, it was that and all, Mr Jones ferry, as nice a little meeting as we've had.' The speaker had taken no part in the music. If it were possible I would have judged that he had slept through it. He had

162

enjoyed more than his share of the beer, and his speech was slurred. Having made the point, he shut his eyes and gave himself to his own thoughts for the rest of the journey. Only when the train came to its abrupt halt did he slide from the seat and sit in a pool of spilled beer until his friends pulled him, uncomplaining, to his feet.

'Some of them's getting on like, Mr Jones. Not so young either, did you notice? On his two sticks Mr Williams post-office is, isn't he then?' The speaker was not so young himself: seventy if he was a day. 'Another small bottle, Mr Hughes, if the opener's handy, thank you.'

'No trouble, Mr Davies, no trouble at all.'

'Settle up at the next meeting, mind.'

'If we have to rob the collection plate in chapel, see,' said a big steaming man with a wink at me. He perhaps felt I was being left out of things. With a hand like a baseball glove he wiped the biggest moustache that surely ever grew on upper lip.

At this point the engine started picking up speed for the final assault on Prestatyn. Urging one another to 'finish up', 'wash it down', 'you'll not waste it, lad, for pity's sake', the boys started getting ready to face the life of every day. They mopped their heads, straightened their ties in the stiff but crumpled collars which met over brass studs of antiquated make, pulled down their waistcoats, attended to their braces, and adjusted their hats and caps. Whippets and band instruments were lowered to the floor, watches were compared at the end of their gilt chains, pipes were knocked out, and an innumerable quantity of bottles were put into the long cardboard boxes which took up most of the space in the corridor.

While all this was going on, my mind dwelled on the mystery of advancing age. Wherever they had spent the day, and whatever the nature of their meeting, here was a trainload of elderly men who, because they had repeated the ritual year after year, were seeing one another as boys. Even as I was reflecting on this quite common phenomenon, and as if to confirm my conclusion, Mr Jones ferry enquired of Mr Davies trumpet who the young man was at the meeting who had sat next to Mr Williams post-office. 'It'd never be his *son*, Mr Davies, would it? Not that big lad: finished school by the looks of him.' The knowing Mr Hughes cut in with 'Ivor? That's Dai Williams's grandson.'

It was still raining when we arrived, but this in no way diminished the joviality of the passengers who poured out of the three carriages on to the platform. There was a lot of farewell handshaking and back-slapping, and as I passed one group on my way to the barrier I heard someone ask Mr Hughes how a Roman Catholic clergyman had come to be one of his party. 'Not so loud, lad, the old gentleman's just behind you.'

Me — *old*?

BED AND BREAKFAST

Ring and walk right in said the hand-printed notice stuck with transparent tape to the front-door of the Beach View Private Hotel. So I did.

The moment I came into the room I knew that he hated priests. He was sitting with his feet on a chair reading *Photoplay*. He had on a singlet through which could be seen a cushion of hair; a pair of shiny brown trousers covering muscular thighs and calves; and a pair of grey imitation suède shoes. No socks. In a fleshy sort of way he was good looking. Between thirty-five and forty? – something like that. Another five years and he would be paunchy. Already he was a bit too thick about the neck, and there were slight puffy bulges where the strap of his wrist-watch was too tight for him. His eyes, pale and of no particular colour, were too close together to inspire confidence. Tattoo marks showed on the white above both elbows; vigorous ginger hair grew below. I wondered if the appearance of health was misleading, and if the pink of his complexion might not be blood-pressure. It was not sunburn. He was an indoor man.

As I could not be sure that this was the proprietor of the Beach View Private Hotel, I put down my suitcase and typewriter and walked across the room to where there was a desk on which there were a telephone, a bell such as you get on the tables in tea shops, a ledger-type book which I took to be a register of names, and a rectangular panel proclaiming *Reception*. I hit the bell with the flat of my hand.

'Yes?' said the man over the top of *Photoplay*.

'I would like a room for the night if you have got one. For three nights in fact.'

'We are full up.'

I am always having to revise judgments of this sort, but I felt certain from the way he held his cigarette, from his quick return to the magazine, from the angle of his freckled hand, that he was lying.

'Don't be daft, Wilf,' said a strong female voice from the other side of a door which stood half-open on the far side of the front room, 'you know what we've got empty. We need the money so shut your big mouth.'

The words were not spoken angrily; more with laughing raillery. It was a good voice.

She came through the door threading a length of elastic through a pair of child's green cotton shorts. She was a good bit younger than Wilf, twenty-three at most. A girl. She looked as strong as a horse. Capable and jolly.

'Just bed and breakfast or full board?' she asked without looking at her husband. She pushed the register across the desk, flicked out a ball-point pen with one hand, and, pointing with the other to the space where I was to sign, unhooked a key which was hanging with its heavy metal label to a board, and went on threading the shorts.

'Bed and breakfast, please. For three days unless you've got people coming.'

'Nobody's coming. There's only two lodgers just now, and both permanents. There's loads of room all week.'

Her husband threw down his magazine, pressed out his cigarette in a few impatient jabs against the sole of his shoe, and stood up. He seemed about to say something, something explosive, but decided against. Instead he picked up a blue flannel blazer which was lying over the back of a chair, and slung it over his shoulders. I am always interested in what people wear when they go out: it shows what kind of image they want to create. The blazer was a vulgar one with red, blue, and white braid round the edges — arranged diagonally and making it look like an airmail envelope — suggesting that the wearer wanted to be taken for one of the boys. The gesture of slinging one's jacket (I belong to a generation which calls it a coat) over one's shoulder is designed to be defiant. Wilf's flourish was not so much combative as childish. To me it seemed the act of a small boy throwing back a towel past his ears and pretending it was an assassin's cloak. The door banged, and the proprietor of the Beach View Private Hotel was out in the street.

'Nice man to have,' she laughed without malice, 'but bad for business. I'll show you your room.'

We went upstairs.

166

'No running water in the rooms, I'm afraid, but a bathroom on the landing. Here's yours, number four, and there's a gas fire if you want it. You put a shilling in the meter and turn on. Next to you, in number three, is Mrs Wicker. You'll have to look out with her. She talks.'

'I have no secrets.'

'I don't mean that. I mean she talks on and on.'

'There are a lot of Mrs Wickers about. I'll manage.'

She laughed.

'The only other one is Charlie Moss, a boy who's studying for something, and he's upstairs because it's cheaper for him. He'll give you no trouble. Just the three of you.'

The room might have been worse. It was clean anyway. The window looked on to a side street. The view of the beach was reserved for the public rooms, and for Mr and Mrs Gates who evidently — as they had every right to do since they were there all the year round — occupied the best bedroom. After unpacking, and noting with some dismay that Mrs Wicker had staked out a generous claim in the bathroom, I went downstairs with the intention of doing some shopping before the shops closed. It was about five in the afternoon. Crossing the hall on the way out I noticed a girl leaning against the open door through which Mrs Gates had spoken to her husband on my arrival. The girl whispered something which I could not hear, and Mrs Gates appeared holding a teapot.

'In a hurry?' she asked, 'because we're having tea in here if you want some.'

I did not want tea but accepted the invitation. I was curious to know if the disagreeable Mr Gates had come back and how he would welcome my presence at his tea. He was still out.

'My kid sister Sandra,' said Mrs Gates indicating the girl, 'and this character with jam on his face is Tom, my little boy. Now you've seen all of us. There'll be another coming before long as you'll have noticed.'

I had not noticed, and was surprised at such frankness. Now that she had mentioned it there was no mistaking her condition, but I did not feel that it called for comment. I asked how old Tom was.

'Three and a bit, aren't you, Tom? And Sandra's sixteen. It's the

167

worst age for a girl: nothing but boys and pop records.'

'Watch it, Jean,' said Sandra.

Sandra was not as smiling a person as her sister. She was as good-looking but slimmer, and dressed in what must be the uniform of her age and kind: jeans, white socks, loose-fitting sweater, low-heeled 'casuals'. Her fair hair, unbrushed and hanging anyhow, was worn long. She held herself badly, giving the impression of laziness and sulkiness — a false impression. When she sat down she did so like a boy.

Tom, at three and a bit, was nothing much either way.

Conversation was not difficult, the topic being Mrs Wicker and Charlie Moss. Sandra revealed, under her sister's gentle teasing, a likeable good humour which gave as much as it got. The six years which separated them made little difference, and anyone listening with his eyes closed might have mistaken the one for the other. It was difficult to believe that Mrs Gates was Tom's mother: she must have been married at eighteen.

While we were talking, and I must have been there for nearly an hour, Charlie Moss came in and we were introduced. He was a long pale boy with a frown and glasses, and I would have dismissed him as the earnest scholar (which he also was) had he not displayed mannerisms which were quite at variance with the stock part of university student and which struck me as amusing. The other two were not allowed to get away with anything, and when apparently cornered he would appeal to me. This I found flattering. Into the congenial atmosphere, to which I found myself unaccountably contributing, came suddenly Mr Gates. But not for long. All he did was to put his head round the door, see who was in the room, throw an evening paper on the table, and go out. I heard him walking upstairs.

'What's biting him then?' asked Sandra.

'You know what he's like,' said Jean.

'All right dinner-time,' commented Charlie Moss.

So my guess had been right: Mr Gates disliked priests.

The reason why one person marries another is always good for a moment's speculation, and I found it easy enough to see how the Gates's had come to be attracted to one another. What I found difficult to understand was how they had managed to stick to one another.

But perhaps I had seen only a surface antagonism in him, and a friendliness in her which might cool on closer acquaintance. No, I told myself, this young woman with her big smoky laugh and her warm tolerant expression was all that she seemed to be.

'You booked for bed and breakfast,' she said when I got up to go, 'but the evening meal's no trouble if you want to stay in. Charlie stays in when he wants to.'

'When he can't pay for it out,' said Sandra, getting in a happy smack.

'Only when I know Sandra's out with a date,' Charlie explained.

'I won't be in this evening, thanks,' I said. I thought I ought to call on the parish priest before he sat down to supper, and make arrangements about Mass in the morning. I would find somewhere to eat. I did not want to embarrass Mr Gates for a third time that day.

The priest was out when I called, so I left a message about Mass. Getting back to the Beach View at the time when they would be having supper, I crept up to my room without seeing anyone. Breakfast would not present the same problem because I would be able to nip in and out and not have to linger in the presence of whoever might be there. Or so I thought.

After writing a few letters and performing my devotions I lay in bed reading the current issue of *Monastic Studies* waiting for my sleeping-pill to work. At about ten I heard Charlie Moss going upstairs to his attic, and a little later I heard Mrs Wicker clip-clopping past my door and letting herself in to number three.

The walls were thin, and perhaps she did not know she had a neighbour, but Mrs Wicker did not keep her movements secret. She crossed the room on firm heels, switched on the wireless which first croaked and then whistled and then slid into dance music, threw herself into a chair which set up a jangle of springs, and kicked off her shoes. I pictured her sitting with her eyes closed, breathing gently and giving herself to rest. Evidently not yet, because the wireless was switched off and the springs yielded up their burden. Drawers were pulled and shot back, clothes-hangers fell to the floor, and curtains clacked on what must have been wooden rings and a wooden rod. And so it went on. There was business with drawing a cork, and some more business of moving furniture. I took another sleeping-pill.

169

Through the night of pleasantly drugged sleep, sounds as of a bird in a wastepaper-basket came to me from next door. Muted scratchings, fussy and restless, belonging to a different species. I got up early, so as to have first go at the bath, and while I shaved I indulged a favourite habit of reconstructing a Mastodon from a knuckle-bone. Assembling the information given to me the evening before about Mrs Wicker, and adding to it the unsolicited evidence which had come through the dividing wall, I had plenty of material to hand. It would be interesting to compare, if we should meet at breakfast, my composition with the original. What had Jean, Sandra and Charlie told me about her? That she was talkative, elderly (whatever that meant, coming from the lips of the young), a figure of fun. She had been on the stage ('and don't she let you know it' — Sandra), was interested in high fashion, had ideas about food. She was not, despite her Shakespearean pretensions, an intellectual. I recalled some of yesterdays talk:

Charlie: 'She gives herself airs about the legitimate stage and that, but she's as dumb as they come. I'll bet she hasn't read a book for years. *Good Companions* maybe.'

Jean: 'But she's sharp enough to see through *you*, Charlie lad, and don't forget it.'

Sandra: '*And* she's the only one to handle our Wilfrid Gates. You have to be clever as a barrel full of monkeys for that if you ask me.' Charlie had laughed immoderately at this, asking if it was a saying or if she had made it up. He said Mrs Wicker was indeed a family of astute little jabbering apes such as you see carved in wood, each one possessed of a lower cunning than its neighbour. 'Never heard the saying before?' Sandra had asked, 'and you call yourself a student. No, I didn't make it up, it's just a saying like wise as an owl and all those.'

Myself: 'But less accurate, because only the monkeys on top would be clever: the others would be fools to let themselves get pushed to the bottom.'

Sandra: 'Sayings aren't meant to be worked out that far.'

Charlie: 'Mrs Wicker's well on top of the barrel anyway, and means to stay there.'

This conversation was, to borrow from the American courtroom scene, exhibit A. For exhibit B there was my own witness: from the bathroom array of bottles, sprays, brushes, tubes I could testify to a hypochondriac and beauty specialist; from a night spent in the adjoing room, there was evidence of an insomniac.

So when I got back from Mass to find only Mr Moss in the diningroom I was faintly disappointed. I took it that Mrs Wicker, with her theatrical background, wanted a good entry — even for breakfast.

Sure enough, no sooner had Sandra brought the coffee and toast than in came the star. She was more than I had hoped for but quite different from what I had expected. Sandra, who had changed from yesterday's blue jeans into tartan trousers, winked at me as she went off to fetch a tray for Mrs Wicker. Charlie had a book in front of him which he now arranged in such a way as to allow him a view of both Mrs Wicker and myself while he remained hidden. I was obviously expected to play up or be played up to.

Working downwards from the top, her hair, which was daffodil yellow in colour, was arranged in a complication ranging from small waves to considerable billows. How much of it was her own I could not tell, but it was not a wig. A little black velvet bow peeped between two major undulations, giving to the whole a certain skittishness which was reflected elsewhere in the plan of her appearance. Quite half an inch above the line of her original eyebrows, now removed but showing still the faintest smudge, was pencilled a reddish-brown pair of curves which made her look habitually surprised. Since her false eyelashes were black, the transition from gold was rendered less sharp by the henna in between. Her pancake make-up was helped out by a rosy flush high on the cheek, a crimson cupid-bow mouth, and shell-pink dabs at the lobes of her ears. I was glad I had got up early to claim the bathroom: all this must have taken a long time to do.

When not talking, though this was seldom if there happened to be anyone in the room, Mrs Wicker held her lips pressed close together in a fixed and knowing smile. The mouth went down at the centre and up at the corners, the sharpness of the angle suggesting much practice. Over each corner hung a rounded fold of cheek, producing the effect of a curtain drawn back and held up in a generous swag, while below the line of the chin — an uncertain line now — the neck fell away in a gentle ripple to be caught from further cascade by a narrow silk ribbon with a small silver-mounted central stone. This

171

black band had the effect of cutting off her face from the rest of her — an impression which, since the stiffly upholstered torso remained rigid and upright while the head, earrings swinging, ceaselessly turned and nodded as though on springs, gained ground with every utterance — and was reminiscent of the old-fashioned domestic Turkish bath where only the bather's head appeared through a hole in the top of the box.

Her boldly flowered dress was far more *jeune fille* than what was worn by either Jean or Sandra, her heels higher, her waist slimmer. Her nails matched her lips; her fingers, knotted with rheumatism, were heavy with rings; veins traced a serpentine pattern on the backs of her hands which were as transparent as grease-proof paper; wrinkles made irregular circles round her bare elbows. She must have been nearer seventy than sixty.

She made a good photographic study as she sat sideways at the table, lightly tapping a cigarette against her silver-plated case as she would have learned to do in the twenties for the drawing-room comedy. When she had got me into focus she tucked her legs, careful not to cross them, under her chair and turned on the spotlight.

In no time I was 'dear', and a few minutes later 'darling'. Charlie, behind his barricade, was enjoying himself, and Sandra, when she came in with Mrs Wicker's chopped carrots and grapefruit juice, raised her eyes to heaven. Mrs Wicker spoke fast, each word articulated, in a voice which had been groomed for special service. I wondered what the original accent had been. Under the eau-de-Cologne there was a Midlands whiff.

Nothing fortunately was expected of me: the monologue was without demand. Even so, I found it exhausting. It was like listening to a bird fluttering against a window-pane: you felt you ought to do something, but if you opened the window you might have the feathers brushing against your face. It was Sandra who came to the rescue in the end. No opening the window for her.

'You're wanted on the phone, mister or father or whatever you are,' she shouted from the kitchen interrupting the speech in the middle of a line.

'And you're telling lies, my girl,' Mrs Wicker shouted back, 'but a hint's a hint, and no offence.'

It gave me my cue and I was up to my room in a flash.

I had hardly settled down to my typewriter, anxious to get my diary up to date while the material (from which all this has been taken) was hot, when Sandra came into the room. Without knocking, I may add. She carried, in a detached way, a broom, and brush and pan, a marigold flannel duster with red stitching.

'You've made your bed anyway,' she said.

'If you want to do the room,' I said, 'I'll go and play with Tom. Tom seems a nice chap. I must get to know him better. He didn't talk much yesterday.'

'No hurry about the room. Not for me, because Charlie does for himself upstairs, and her ladyship in number three likes me to do hers when she goes out for her morning pint.'

She leaned the broom against the chest of drawers, put the other things down, and sat on the bed. She asked me what I was writing.

'I was going to write up my diary,' I said, 'but can't remember a word that woman said at breakfast. Can you?'

'It's always like that. Never stops and nothing at the end of it. Look, what are you doing here? We don't get your sort coming here ordinarily.'

She put her head on one side, and, quite without the archness of Mrs Wicker, studied me through half-closed eyes.

'I'm filling in time. Why?'

'You're not a cop?'

'You watch too much television.'

'You type a lot. Maybe you're writing a book?'

'So it was you who went through my papers when I was out last night? I didn't think it was your sister.'

She blushed.

'I wanted to see if it was a disguise. You weren't like a priest somehow.'

'Others have told me the same thing. There doesn't seem much I can do. Anyhow I am one.'

'O.K., O.K., I believe you. Even so, what's a priest doing at Beach View? Just on holiday?'

'I got some dates wrong, if you must know, and arrived at a convent three days before I was supposed to. I didn't want to be a nuisance to the nuns, so arranged to come back in three days' time. And now, as I told you, I'm filling in time. Satisfied?'

'O.K., O.K., I believe you. Do you think I'd be a good nun?'

'No.'

Sandra went about her duties, and I spent most of the day in the public library. At about teatime I came back to the hotel, and as I went up the stairs to my room I heard Gates walking out, slamming the front door. He must have seen me from the kitchen or the private room leading off the hall.

'There's tea going downstairs if you want it,' said either Jean's or Sandra's voice outside my door. Their voices were alike, but it was probably Jean's because there had been a knock. I said I would be down.

The television was on when I joined them — a commercial advertising a happy and thoughtful dental cream, a loving family cream which would not let you down at a party — and they did not switch it off. Jean was drying her hair with a rough towel, and went on drying it. Charlie and Sandra were there, sitting where they had sat the day before. I was expected, taken for granted.

When she had finished rubbing her hair, Jean dropped the towel in a damp lump on Tom's head and went to work with her fingers. She threw her head back and shook it, still running one hand through the thick hair while with the other she poured hot water into the teapot. A quick comparison flashed through my mind between this and the studied unselfconsciousness of the old lady upstairs.

During the hour that I was there I observed how each of those present was effortlessly engaged in being true to type. Tom sucked at, but did not finish, a thick slice of bread and jam which he held absentmindedly to various parts of his face while watching the television screen. ('We leave it on for him most of the day,' Jean told me, 'but turn down the sound. He doesn't understand the sound part anyway.') Charlie helped with the tea-things and made swift amusing comments on every topic. He showed himself well informed but not assertively so, and it turned out he was a Communist. For his Communist sympathies he was attacked with more traditional prejudice than reasoning by Jean and Sandra. In argument he lost none of his good humour but on the contrary made fun of what he called Beach

View bourgeoisie and of the medieval superstitions of twentieth-century Rome. 'I don't mind your being an anachronism,' he told me, 'but it's the limit when you Roman Catholics preach about all other anachronisms being wrong. We Communists are anachronisms too: we belong to the future.' 'Oh, pack it up,' said Sandra.

'You in for supper, Charlie?' Jean asked.

'If that's O.K., Mrs G.'

'I'll be out,' I said. I thought that if Mr Gates were present I would be either rude or artificially amicable, and I did not want to be one or the other.

'Too bad because you'll miss Maxime,' said Jean with a chuckle, 'who's a friend of Mrs Wicker's. She was an actress too, but in variety. And a lot of fun.'

'Brother, when they two get together,' said Sandra.

'It's like *Those Were the Days.* I'm glad I'm staying in,' said Charlie. 'Talk about anachronisms,' he added.

'I'm glad I'm not home; they drive me nuts.'

'You going out then, Sandra?'

'Rod and I are going to *Tom Jones.*'

'I hope you know it's an X film,' I said.

'O.K., so what?'

'It makes her feel big to go to X films,' Charlie explained, 'our big sophisticated Sandra, mature woman of the world.'

'Nice and adult yourself, aren't you, Mr grown-up-schoolboy Moss.'

'Give it a rest, you two,' said Jean, and turning to me: 'It wears you down, doesn't it, listening to this all day.'

'It's his crazy ideas, Jean, that start me off. I don't try and push him around. I got troubles enough. So he better not push me around.'

She went out. Jean shrugged her shoulders. Tom, without removing his eyes from the television screen, ran a forefinger down the middle of his bread and jam and put what he had scooped up into his mouth.

'She was going out anyway to change,' said Charlie to nobody in particular.

'Tell me about Maxime,' I asked.

Charlie, Jean and I washed up, Charlie was laying the tables in the dining-room when I left the house for a visit to the church.

175

That evening I had sandwiches and coffee at a snack-bar in the High Street. It was September and the summer visitors were thinning out. I enjoyed walking along the front as the evening darkened, and wondering at the lives of the holiday-makers. It pleased me to think that the same apparently haphazard confluence of circumstances which had brought me to the Beach View, a confluence which my religious training had taught me to see as far from haphazard, had arranged to have these people here and nowhere else tonight. If I found it amusing to imagine their backgrounds, I hoped they found it equally amusing to imagine mine. I doubt if they would have associated me with the Beach View Hotel. I doubt if I would either — anyway a week ago — yet here was I, transplanted from my normal environment, quite closely associated with it.

So closely, in fact, that I caught myself speeding up my return to be in time to meet Mrs Wicker's guest, Maxime. It was dark when I reached the hotel, and the two old ladies were lingering at their table in candlelight. Sounds of washing-up came from the kitchen. The television was talking away in a Brooklyn accent to an empty living-room: Tom had gone to bed.

'I would like you to meet my friend, Miss D'Arnley, who has been dining with me tonight. Miss Maxime D'Arnley — you will have heard of her. We theatre folk stick together through thick and thin. I have retired from the stage as I think I have told you, but Miss D'Arnley still tops the bill when she goes on tour.' I shook hands with a soft little pincushion, and wondered what bill Miss D'Arnley could possibly top. 'But she's resting at the moment — aren't you, darling?'

'Very pleased to meet you,' said Miss D'Arnley with a too flashing smile, 'I'm sure.'

Maxime was commoner than Mrs Wicker — much. She was also younger — but not much. She was pink and hot and hovering between over-confidence and giggling embarrassment. Though she was clearly not a deep thinker, such thoughts as passed through her mind revealed themselves instantly in her face. What she was thinking now was: do priests like ladies to be frivolous and perhaps a little familiar, or do they prefer ladies who are serious and have difficulties? It could be seen at once that two things were of paramount importance to Miss D'Arnley: femininity and pleasing people. I warmed to her. I could

176

not find it in my heart to blame either of them, Mrs Wicker or her guest, for being a little drunk.

The candlelight, which I took to be part of the ritual of these little suppers, showed the remains of an unevenly balanced meal. Mrs Wicker had nibbled at lettuce and tomato, and there was a glass cup of tinned peaches left half eaten to reveal where conscience had put its foot down, but Maxime had tucked in. A lamb chop on an island of mashed potatoes survived two of its fellows and what must have been a generous hill of potato; there had been meringues and custard, triangles of processed cheese, crisp rolls which made their grey square counterparts on the other side of the table look like coffin-lids. Sandra being out for the evening the plates had been left as they were. The good-natured Charlie, I guessed, was waiting in the pantry to clear and help Jean with the washing-up.

'Would you not care to join us over a glass of port wine?' said Mrs Wicker, as though extending the hospitality of Elsinore.

'I don't think so, thanks, if you'll forgive me. I have work to do, and there's something I want to ask Mrs Gates before I go up.'

'Please yourself, luv,' said Maxime, having arrived at a conclusion as to how ladies might be well advised to address priests, 'it was just a thought.'

'In *that* case,' said Mrs Wicker hurriedly, anxious to prevent her friend from displaying a too expansive comradeship, 'it would be a good idea if we took the bottles upstairs with us.' With a bottle each, leaving a free hand to grasp the friendly banister, the two ladies walked with great precision from the dining-room. 'Mrs G., darling, Maxie and I are taking away the wines. They won't keep, and it seems such a shame to waste them.' This last was said in a voice thrown to the dress circle. I blew out the three candles and switched on the light. I was glad that those two lined and sagging faces had at least been spared the shaming glare. I joined Jean and Charlie in the kitchen.

'I hope they won't keep you awake,' said Jean. 'We get this about once a month, and Maxime stays till midnight nearly. But it's the only fun they have, poor old dears, and they look forward to it.'

'Does Mr Gates mind?' I wished I had not asked. It looked as though I expected him to mind everything.

'Wilf? Takes no notice. They bring their own drink, and it's not as if he had to go out for it. Sandra's the one who minds.'

'Why?'

'Why?' echoed Charlie, 'because Sandra minds everything, that's why.'

I worked hard when I got to my room, and whatever the high-jinks that were going on next door I was able to get to sleep when I had finished. Maxime left well before twelve, and I heard Mrs Wicker filling her hotwater-bottle. Could they possibly have finished between them a bottle of claret and a bottle of port, and yet remained so decorous? I decided that the remains of the port was probably stowed away behind those clothes-hangers which were always falling down.

When I got back from Mass in the morning I had the dining-room to myself. Jean brought me my tray and said that Charlie had breakfasted early and had gone out. Sandra had come home late and was still asleep. Tom, waiting for television to come on, wandered in and out. Tom had a curious way of starting a conversation and leaving it in mid-air. He would ask a question, sit on the chair in front of me as though waiting for the lecture to begin, and then run off. While I was debating within myself whether this tendency derived from hearing Mrs Wicker talk or watching his father refusing to talk, Mrs Wicker herself walked in and sat down. It was not an entry this morning. When she smiled her three-cornered smile at me in greeting I had a quick vision of a porcelain face cracking and falling apart. But when I looked I could see that the pieces were too closely stuck together for such a thing to happen. The lines were clogged with powder and smoothed over. The soft mounds under her eyes and chin drooped a little, but her hair was rigidly in position and every gesture composed. Her body might have been encased in iron — probably was.

After breakfast I went back to the book I was then writing, so it was almost noon when Sandra came in.

'Hallo,' I said, 'how was *Tom Jones*?'

'It didn't shock me if that's what you mean.'

'It's not what I meant, but it doesn't matter.'

'It might have shocked you though — if you really are what you say you are.'

'So you're still on about that.'

'Anyway, how did our show girls behave without me to tell them where they got off?'

'Mrs Wicker and Maxime? I thought they were rather splendid.'

'Why splendid for heaven's sake?'

'Because they are so determined not to give up. Most of us decide before we're half their age that it isn't worth it, but they're just bashing on. Look at you: you've more or less thrown your hand in already.'

'Hey.'

She put down her broom and the other things, and sat on the bed. She looked a lot more tired than Mrs Wicker, and for a moment I thought she was going to stretch out and go to sleep. I would not have put it beyond her. She was still thinking of Mrs Wicker and her guest, not of the pompous little homily I had delivered about keeping the flag flying.

'Did they give you that bit —' here she imitated the Wicker voice — 'it's a pity to waste it so we might as well take it upstairs.'

'I found it rather touching.'

'You would. You're as bad as Jean. Jean lets them all get away with it. Charlie and Wilf included. Why ever she married Wilf beats me. Doesn't it you?'

'I've met him only briefly. Once when I arrived, and a few times on the stairs. He doesn't seem a terribly communicating person, certainly, whereas she obviously is.'

'He's as mean as hell.'

That afternoon I came to tea without being asked. I might have been born in the Beach View Private Hotel. When we broke up — Sandra was going out again so left early to dress — I suggested to Charlie that unless he meant to stay in we might meet somewhere for supper. (Apparently dinner was for the middle of the day.) So it was arranged that he would pick me up at the church in two hours' time. 'I know of a place,' he said, 'just right for anachronisms.'

'You and your anachronisms,' said Jean, putting the loaf in a tin.

Arriving punctually, Charlie showed none of the non-Catholic's discomfort at being in a Catholic church. He was interested in the confessional and the holy-water stoup. He had seen a font before. I wondered if he had ever been held over one. But we were not in the

179

church for long because he said the place he had in mind might be filling up at this hour.

The restaurant did not greatly impress me when we got there, but it was his choice so I let him have it. It was pretentiously dark for one thing, lit only by would-be exotic table-lamps. The ceiling was low, modelled in a series of rounded arches which were meant to suggest the wine-cellar. A counter, running from the door to the back wall, was supported by a line of large varnished barrels. On the counter were a cash-register, a glass case containing a wide variety of chocolate bars, and a row of black wine bottles turned into lamp-stands. False candles were screwed to the neck of the bottles, splashing a lavish splutter of false wax down the bottles' sides. These lamps were for sale, so were not turned on. Bottle-ends appeared in rows, let into the wall, over both the doorway and the windows. The scene — particularly since patrons could order only tea, coffee, and soft drinks with their meal — lacked conviction.

Through this dim cavern the waitresses flitted with their trays of poached egg and baked beans, and every now and then a troglodyte, tired of waiting, would rise from his table and put a coin in the jukebox and we would hear a sixpenny snatch of Mersey beat.

'Funny place you've brought me to,' I said to Charlie who was studying the menu card.

'Aye?' he said absently, 'well, it makes a change . . . and it's better than most.'

'Oh, I'm sure,' I said, 'and bung over that card when you've finished with it.'

'Pardon?'

'I said "bung over" which belongs to the idiom of my youth. When I am out of my element like this, I tend to reach back into the past for a rope to haul on. You probably have a vocabulary to describe the room we are in — 'cool' or 'fab' or something — so you won't mind if I call it a pretty footling sort of place. Now tell me about your landlord and mine, Mr Wilfrid Gates.'

'He's O.K., I suppose, but he doesn't take to everybody. He's had a hard time, in the army and that. He was still only a kid when he was caught by the Japs and given the full treatment. That's probably the explanation. Often he doesn't seem quite normal.'

'I'm glad you told me.'

A little waitress in black-and-white came swimming towards us through the drifts of cigarette smoke which hung horizontally in broken layers above the tables. We stopped her, and Charlie ordered sausages for himself, sardines for me. We were going to make a night of it.

Hardly had the waitress disappeared behind the expresso jet, which momentarily drowned the jukebox, when I noticed another young woman bearing down upon us.

'Look who's here,' said Sandra.

It was hardly surprising that I had not recognized her. Having seen her up till now wearing jeans or trousers, I was not prepared for the skirt and well-cut jacket. The costume was simple, with sleeves reaching just above her wrists, and of a cornflower blue which, even in the sepulchral gloom of the cave, brought out the colour of her eyes. Her hair was brushed smooth, and she had chosen a shade of lipstick which matched her bright red bag and patent-leather high-heeled shoes. Stockings, a little silk handkerchief tucked into a gilt bracelet, white cotton gloves. Dazzling as all this was, I infinitely preferred the Sandra of the brush and pan.

'Gosh,' I said as she swung a chair from the next table and sat down, 'you've fairly laid it on. I didn't know you. Charlie, did you recognise her?'

'I've seen her like this before. I suppose she's trying to look like Mrs Wicker.'

'You do enjoy spoiling everything, don't you?' said Sandra with some heat. 'Give me a cigarette.'

Charlie patted his pockets and threw a crumpled packet on the table but did not come forward with a light. As she lit her cigarette I noticed how her schoolgirl fingers, bitten and unvarnished nails, were less expert than she would have wished.

'How old are you, Sandra?' I asked. I knew already.

'Sixteen. Now don't *you* start.'

'I'm sorry. Look, what are you having to eat? If you promise not to quarrel with Charlie, who is in a bad mood anyway, you can have my sardines when they come. I'll order some more.'

'You can keep your sardines. I'm at another table and we're having the *table d'hote*. Me and my friend. *Table d'hote.*'

The repetition was for her own satisfaction, not for ours.

When Charlie had come to pick me up at the church he was already in a bad mood. The Vat Café-Grille had done nothing to raise his spirits.

'My friend's making signs, so I'd better be going back,' said Sandra, 'be seeing you.'

I watched her winding her way between the tables on her high heels. There was nothing boyish about her movements now. Nor was she showing off. It was just the difference which clothes make at that age. I was interested to see what her friend would be like, so when she reached her table I had a good look. The light from the table-lamp fell full upon a young man whose appearance did not impress me. He wore rings on both hands and a shining silk tie with a knot the size of a sandwich. Dark oiled hair swept forward over his forehead almost to his nose, while at the sides it was combed back in an arrangement of waves. He was a frowning young man, pallid rather than sallow, and too square for the elegance which the apparatus of his appearance was designed to present. Since what lay beyond the yellow pool of light was hidden from view I was prevented from studying him further.

'So that, I suppose, is Rod.'

'Actually it's Stan,' said Charlie, without looking round to see. He was flicking the packet of cigarettes from one hand to the other across the table. 'But they're all the same, her dates. They are what *you* would call bounders or stinkers or something like that. They don't do anyone much good, that lot. Someone ought to tell her to grow up. She's just a kid.'

'You're in love with her aren't you, Charlie?'

He nodded but did not look up. His eyes followed the backwards and forwards movement of the packet of cigarettes as though he were at Wimbledon. I turned from him to the more distant contemplation of Sandra, a mere blurr of blue against the imitation brick. The uncertain outline told me nothing. As it turned out, for the two must have left shortly afterwards, this was the last I saw of Sandra. Next morning, when I moved from the Beach View to the convent, she was not yet down.

'I see why you chose this joke place to come to this evening,' I said, 'though you haven't had much fun out of it.'

'I'll marry her in four years from now.' He stopped playing with his cigarettes, and looked at me. 'You don't believe that do you?'

'Funnily enough I think I do. Send me a card, and if I'm still alive I'll come to the ceremony. If Communists have ceremonies, that is. I hope you'll both be very very happy. Here come the sausages and sardines.'

He looked at the plates as though they were piled high with wedding rings and orange-blossom, and for the rest of the meal he was in a good mood.

So much for our party at the Vat Café-Grille.

Next day, when I paid my bill, Jean said she hoped I would come again. 'Next time you must get to know Wilf more. I don't know what's come over him these last few days. He gets like that but it's never anything personal.'

'I understand perfectly.' I did not.

Tom gave me his left hand to shake. I left farewell messages for Mrs Wicker and Sandra. Charlie had come to my room on his way out and had said goodbye rather shyly as I was getting my things into the suitcase. I came away unwillingly from the Beach View Private Hotel.

At the convent, where I was assured on arrival that I had got the date right this time, I ran into the parish priest who was calling on the reverend mother. Hitherto I had met him only in the sacristy after either his Mass or mine.

'I wish I had known,' he said, 'you could have stayed with me. It was a pity I was out when you came the first time. I hope you found a nice hotel.'

I told him I had found a most suitable hotel, a modest establishment on the sea-front called the Beach View Private Hotel. Perhaps he knew it?

He looked surprised. 'I have never been inside, but I know the place you mean. Unfortunate that you should have hit on that particular hotel. It's run by someone called Wilfrid Gates.'

'Well, she does most of the running. He's a rum chap, not awfully friendly, but the others in the household couldn't have been more amiable. Gates was beaten up, it seems, in a prisoner-of-war camp before he took on this hotel job.'

'Before he took on *any* job. Father Gates was a priest of this diocese.'

LOCAL TIME

The subject of what follows is someone whose name I do not know, whose age must be about thirteen, whose appearance suggests the country rather than the town, and whose accent, though I met her in Wales, is English. Moreover she is one whose concern with current fashions in dress is either not yet awakened or else highly chic at the present time. It was her intelligence, shining and quick, which stirred me. A few generations ago she would have been invented by Saki, given a clipped diction by Mr Noel Coward, and put into a plot by Mr Maugham. Who can say what will happen to her now? Even if she leaves no mark on the public, she is going to be more than a handful for somebody.

For a week or more a problem had been wrapping itself round my head like a tight bandage. A Chinese philosopher, writing in the fourteenth century, said that when this happens the thing to do is to buy a horse or build a house. In my case the facilities were lacking; I decided to go for a long walk and so tire myself out. Hardly had I started when a car drove up from behind me, slowed down, and I was offered a lift. Having no specific destination in mind I was able to get myself dropped where I pleased, so, having crossed from Flintshire to Denbighshire and finding the countryside harmless, I asked to be put down on the road somewhere between Henllan and Denbigh.

I walked for two hours, at the end of which I was lost. Whenever I came to a new road I took it. My problem was no nearer solution; the bandage was, if anything, tighter. So it was that when a voice spoke to me from over a farm gate, it spoke as if from another planet. The words were carefully articulated, equal stress being given to each syllable. Had another been present I would have assumed some sort of game. Since there was nobody there but the speaker, the joke must have been a purely private one. On reflection, the joke must have been myself. The opening was unremarkable.

'Excuse me. Can you' (pointing at me) 'tell me' (pointing to herself) 'the right time?'

'I can tell you the *wrong* time,' I said, looking at my watch which I saw had stopped, 'and I see it is just ten past ten. It would have been right, I should say, about two hours ago. I can give you a lot of other wrong times as well, because there are so many more to choose from than the right ones, but I doubt if they would be much use to you.'

'You mean I could find out what they were just as well as you could? That midnight, for instance, is one of the times it isn't?'

'Exactly,' I said, 'you get my meaning perfectly.'

She was swinging slowly backwards and forwards on the gate, her feet on a lower bar and her hands resting on the top one. She was wearing a pair of old blue jeans, a dark brown sweater with a roll-over collar which came up to her ears, no socks, a pair of worn gymshoes. Her eyes were brown, set far apart and possibly too big for the rest of her face which was small and sunburned. A distinctive feature was her hair which some would have called red; it was more the colour of rich deep marmalade. It was cut short round the neck like a boy's, hanging in a ragged fringe over her forehead.

'The thing is,' she said, 'do you think it is time I fed my pets?'

'I doubt it. Unless they are seagulls who have very small insides and apparently need food every sixteen minutes. This is a piece of information which will be invaluable to you in after life. Do you in fact keep seagulls?'

'Dragons.'

In swaying backwards and forwards she gave a particular character to anything she said. When leaning back, away from the gate, she looked at me through half-closed eyes; when leaning forward her eyes rounded to a stare. The former was for enquiry, the latter for statement. 'Dragons' was said from the forward position.

'How stupid of me,' I said, 'I should have guessed of course. Denbighshire is the very home of dragons. Tell me about yours.'

'That's not fair. You were expected to show surprise.'

'Begin again and I'll try. But perhaps I've lived too long to feel surprise.'

'How long?'

186

'Fifty-nine years.'

'Fifty-nine, fifty-nine . . . the average age of a porcupine. What does it feel like being fifty-nine?'

'Ask an average porcupine.'

'Hooray. I *knew* you were going to say that. I knew, I knew. We can finish with porcupines now, so you just tell me. What does it feel like? Go on. Honestly. I want to know.'

It is not often that a line of Shakespeare comes into my head, but I remembered that 'her voice was ever soft, gentle and low'. Why should a man remember a play which he has not read for years and forget completely a problem that has been on his mind for days?

'People will give you different answers, but since you ask me I find it feels exactly the same as being thirteen or fourteen or whatever you are. That's just the hard part because you are expected to be something else altogether. That's the catch about growing up – you don't.'

'What a pity. I thought everything would change. You know, I was thinking about growing up when I saw you coming along. You looked so long and serious, all dressed in black. I said to myself: "Here comes the most grown-up person I've ever seen; I'll ask him what it's like." '

'So you didn't really want to know the time at all. In that case you had better give it back. On second thoughts I gave you the wrong one so you needn't bother. What beats me is that if you wanted to start up a conversation you should choose such a boring subject to do it with.'

'I might have asked you if you had a lawn-mower on you which I could borrow for a minute . . . or what was the date of the Battle of Waterloo . . . or how to tell the difference between a mushroom and a toadstool.'

She went on swinging backwards and forwards, looking me over as though I were a dragon in a pet-shop. I could hardly object to her studying me since I was studying her. So it was on grounds of security that I protested.

'Don't keep doing that or you'll fall off. Besides it's rude to stare. What do you think I am—a seagull? a porcupine?'

'I think,' she said, her brown eyes narrowing as she continued her rhythmic movement as though I had made no reference to it. 'I

187

think . . . I think' (swing) 'you're funny.'

It was months since I had spoken to any young people, so perhaps the observation struck me as being older than in fact it was. Why should an elderly stranger of forbidding aspect appear funny? Was this just her idea or would other people, most people, think me funny?

'Perhaps it's you who's funny,' I said, 'and not me at all. I don't feel a bit funny.'

'You don't have to *feel* funny to *be* funny.'

'In other words you think it's like growing up. You either are or are not.'

'Too complicated. Tell me a story, please.'

'I know only one and it's got a sad ending. You tell me one.'

'I tell myself stories, but I never tell stories to other people in case it spoils them. Mine never have sad endings.'

'I'll bet they don't.'

'Can you guess why not?'

'Tell me.'

'Because they never have any endings at all.'

'Those kind are the best. There are one or two good ones like that in the Bible. The secret of literature is to keep people guessing. I won't bore you with a sermon, but the secret of religion is a bit like that too — with one important difference. I bore very easily.'

'Not if I made up my mind to unbore.'

'We must leave the experiment for another day. Listen, can you tell me the right road to Denbigh?'

'I know what I'm expected to say. I'm expected to give you a lot of *wrong* roads to Denbigh. As it happens you are on the *right* road to Denbigh, but in the direction you're going you would have to go all the way round the world and come in to Denbigh from the other side. You'd have to go through India and China and all those places. But it might be worth it. You never know.'

'I'll keep straight on then, and send you a postcard from the Taj Mahal.'

'Too much like school.'

'Goodness,' I said, 'if it's like the Taj Mahal you must go to a very grand school.'

At this she raised her eyes to heaven and made a despairing gesture with her shoulders.

'Too much like what we *learn* at school. *Hon*estly.'

'And talking about that, how is it you're not at school now? Oughtn't you to be? The term is still on, isn't it?'

'I'm terribly ill,' she said, leaning far back and looking as healthy as a pippin, 'so I'm not allowed to risk it. Sad, don't you think?'

'Leprosy?'

'Galloping.'

'Goodbye.'

'Goodbye, I was right, you're funny.'

I did not look back. It never does to look back. But I knew she was there because I could hear the gate creaking at regular intervals. It must have been long past the feeding time for those dragons.

It is no good worrying about girls with freckles on their hands who swing on gates, and wondering what will happen to them. But one worries all the same. I kept on walking — towards India and China and all those places.

FLINTSHIRE SAFARI

Summer in North Wales is normally cold and wet. This year however there was one singing week of sunshine which drew most of us out of doors. Only on the brightest and hottest days do I feel the urge to walk, so it was almost as a compliment to Wales that I decided to move on foot from Talacre to Rhyl and see how the sea was getting on. My holiday mood carried me past caravan sites, novelty shops, snack-bars, pin-table casinos, beach photographers, innumerable ice-cream vans, soft drink stalls, a bandstand or two (emptied by the provenance of the transistor), and one rather sad Punch and Judy pitch. Arrived at the throbbing heart of Rhyl, which in summer throbs on the promenade and in winter not at all, I found a bench which was in sight of the sea (though only just, for many places of entertainment screen the view), removed my hat, assured myself that the Royal Floral Hall had not cut off the heating, and addressed my mind to the problem of enjoying myself. With me the joy of being alive seldom lasts longer than seven minutes, and I wondered what I should do next in the effort to keep it going. One does not want to push one's luck in these things, and as I was casting about for new incentives, experience having taught me how suddenly enthusiasm can die, the only other occupant of the bench got up, yawned, handed me his newspaper folded at the middle page, and shuffled out of my life. As though divining my thought, he had provided the incentive. There it was in print on the open page: an account, illustrated with map and photographs, of how a certain Dr Clifford Sears, aged sixty-one, had crossed the Caribbean on a raft. No raft for me, but incentive none the less. I read on.

Dr Sears had designed the raft himself, fitted it together in his own back garden, bought a few things, and taken off. I forget how many weeks he had spent on the water under the open skies. There was no mention in the article of his being in constant radio communication with the mainland. Nothing about rescue teams standing by.

190

He had made a list, a short one, of what medical supplies he thought he would need. There was not a word about being backed by a paper or by cigar-smoking, steak-eating, highball-drinking, eight-hour-a-night-sleeping managers and promoters. Dr Sears had simply shoved off from a particular beach one morning and grounded his craft on the other side of the ocean weeks, or it may have been months, later. (I should have kept the paper but it did not occur to me to do so.)

Earlier in the year I had read of young Canadians shooting rapids on skis, of Frenchmen breaking records for the time they spent in potholes, of Swedes and Norwegians scaling vertical faces of rock, of Americans nipping out of the light of moving glaciers. But these were all young men, born in a commando unit and nursed by a graded scale of assault courses, for whom nature and the elements existed solely to be conquered. Dr Clifford Sears on the other hand was a quiet old stick-in-the-mud like me. In fact three years *older* than me.

It was this last which made me ponder. Here was I feeling pretty pleased with myself for having walked eleven miles from the Abbey to the bench. Also feeling pretty exhausted. How would I look on the high seas, living on hard tack and hauling on heavy ropes all day with old Sears? 'You are getting soft,' I told myself, 'and unless you do something about it you will dodder through your declining years in slippers avoiding draughts.' The prospect so weighed upon me that I forgot the sun, the gleaming sands, the lazy line of heat-wave sea, the sparkle and colour of living.

I put away my glasses, stuffed the newspaper into a wire basket which said 'Post Early for Christmas', and creaked across the road towards the bus terminus. It was then that I saw in the window of a shop which sold equipment an arresting notice TENTS FOR SALE OR HIRE. I went into the shop and explained that I wished to hire a tent.

'Just a single tent, sir?'

'One will be quite enough.'

'What I meant, sir, was to enquire if you wanted the tent for one person or for two.'

'Just for myself, thank you.' I could see from the look he gave me that he thought I was no longer the man for the great outdoors: much much older than Dr Sears.

'Then may I recommend some of the amenities advertised by Camping Comforts Ltd? A pneumatic mattress for instance?'

'I have got a sleeping-bag at home, thank you, so shall not need anything more.'

'Not even a groundsheet, sir? In that case I strongly advise our small self-generating heater which is fitted with a fully tested safety device guarding against fire. You would find it a wise precaution against rheumatism.'

How would Achilles have felt if someone had suggested that as a precautionary measure he put a little pad round the back of his heel?

'If not the heater, sir, then perhaps this table-lamp which carries its own battery, guaranteed three months' service, in the base? No wires to worry about, no danger of a fuse, no need to re-charge. Very comforting if I may say so, sir, that last quiet read to start you off on your night's sleep.'

What would Atlas have said if someone had come along with a crane – just to get the thing up? By now I was tired of the dialogue but the salesman had to live I supposed. He made one final attempt. It had something to do with a washing kit which turned into something else when you placed it upside down. I was not listening, my rejections automatic.

'Ah, the tried campaigner I see –' a pardonable frivolity but it grated – 'and to tell the truth, sir, it is the way I would choose myself. Just the good old-fashioned hurricane lamp, and enough clothes to snuggle down and get comfortable.'

It was too much trouble to explain that the point of the whole thing was *not* to get comfortable.

'Finally, sir, for how *long* were you planning to use the tent? In the case of lengthy hire we make reductions.'

'The short term will suit me,' I said. Dr Sears or no Dr Sears, I was not likely to be under canvas for ever.

'Four days then. Please sign here. Payment in advance, sir, to cover insurance you understand.'

'Just as a matter of interest,' I asked, 'insurance against what?'

'Death and damage,' he replied in his nice brisk salesman voice.

Though I guessed that in this hitch-hiking age a tent could be so packed as to take up little room I was nevertheless surprised at the neatness of my burden. On the bus nobody stared at me as I put the pack among the folded baby-carriages under the stairs. Back along the road I had walked in the morning. Back past Robin Hood Camping Site with Complete Caravan Accommodation (which includes Friar Tuck Tearooms and Maid Marion Beauty Parlour); back past Holiday Hideout with its swimming-pool, inflated Disney-ana, fluorescent signs; back past Kiddie-Kampus with its sandpit and pedal-cars and crying children. After only a few heatwave days everyone was pink, bleached, peeling, swelling, raw-looking. From the bus's top deck I noticed that though the cinemas in Prestatyn were offering both bingo and Mr Burton to their patrons they were attracting little custom. The populace was choosing the glare, the sand, the donkeys, the salt water.

By the time I got back it was too late to do anything about spending that night under canvas. I might have put up the tent, it is true, in the garden at the back of the presbytery. But it seemed a rather ridiculous thing to do. I tried a dress rehearsal, spreading out the material on the dining-room floor, and this at least showed me how is should be assembled. The uneasy suspicion remained however that it is one thing to see a lot of parts lying flat and another to have them standing in position. Another aspect which troubled me was the colour. It was vivid yellow.

Next day, after some difficulty in getting it folded into a portable form, I carried the tent out to a field lying well beyond the Abbey's enclosure and away from houses, caravans and cars. I chose between one and two for this journey because I judged that the world lunched at that hour. It is strange that there are so many people in North Wales who apparently do not want lunch. I did not mind it when Mr Sugden at the lodge waved at me and smiled. He is an old friend and I was able to pass if off. But when, as though released by a factory hooter, men and women thronged by I was put to some confusion by first their curious glances and then their kindly offers of help.

Reaching the place I had selected I spent the best part of two hours setting up my night's shelter. At one point I seriously thought of abandoning the idea of a tent altogether and considered sleeping under the stars. Honour might not allow me to go back on a project, but honour would be more than satisfied if I went one better than a mere scout. At just that moment when I was about to break the collapsable wooden uprights across my knee and tear the canvas to shreds, the tent stood up from the grass firm and proud and yellow. No need now to think of a bivouac. Dr Sears himself probably had some kind of awning over his head most of the time.

The tiresome part over, I went back to the house for the sleeping-bag, books, candles, pyjamas and washing things, sleeping-pills, and tin of biscuits which was to be my supper. I planned to strike camp next morning in time to reach the chapel at the usual hour of five. So it was about six in the evening, the heatwave going full blast, that I pushed up the hill for the second time that day. More heavily laden now than on the earlier ascent, I looked forward to the cool and quiet of my rented tent. Before I reached the brow of the hill I turned and saw Gronant, Prestatyn, and even in the far distance something which might be the outskirts of Rhyl, spread out below me. The sea looked oily and warm, but closer than I had expected. The air was clearer. So clear in fact that I could hear young voices from over the hill.

There were probably no more than four or five little boys in the tent when I arrived but on account of the confined space the number seemed greater. They were disappointed when I explained that they must go away but took it in a philosophical spirit. To them it was simply part of the unfairness of adult behaviour, not to be questioned.

'You an explorer or something?' one little boy asked as he lingered at the flap. He struck me as looking pale and ill until I noticed that his companions looked the same, and that it was the yellow light from the tent.

'In a sort of way,' I replied.

There were some cows in the field, but no other tents, no caravans. That was why I had chosen the site; it was more than most people would have been ready to climb. I said Compline, read a chapter of *Le Milieu Divin,* took a Nembutal, and, blowing out the candle, made a list of the things I had forgotten.

The storm did not break until about midnight. When it did, and with a suddenness which must be very unusual, it seemed to break from everywhere at once. Even from underneath. It was as though something angry were buried immediately under my sleeping-bag and was acting in colusion with the thunder overhead. Meanwhile the frightened lightning was whipping round the tent, too busy to get out of the rain. I was surprised at the way the yellow tent resisted the rain. More accurately I was surprised that I had made it secure enough to resist the rain. By rights the whole thing, myself inside it, should be floating down towards Gronant on a great rush of wave. With the cloudburst had come a change of temperature and I began to think of the small self-generating heater. 'All you have to do is just agitate this little lever (A) at the side – so – until a steady glow appears at the mesh aperture (B).' But it was no good thinking about that. I put my head out into the plunging night and looked at it for a bit. Except when the lightning flashed there was not much to see but there was the feel of it.

Soon the noise died down to an even beating of rain, and water began trickling in. I knew that according to the book I should be outside in oilskins digging a trench to drain the ground near the tent. Lacking oilskins and spade I disposed my mind for further sleep. Between two and three in the morning the rain was still falling but not as heavily as before. What woke me this time was a dull thumping on the canvas as though someone were clubbing a suet pudding to death. It is no easy thing to knock at the door of a tent. Abruptly the thumping stopped, and I heard footsteps squelsh away in the wet.

A little later I was wakened by the light of a passing hurricane-lamp. There seemed to be a lot of traffic on that lonely hillside. Not wanting to miss whatever happened to be going on I had left the tent-flap open, so when the lamp came to a halt I saw, framed in the triangle of the entrance, part of a man's figure. What I could see of him was very wet.

'Can you spare me a minute, please?' said a youthful voice in the unmistakable tones of Liverpool. ('Spur.')

195

'Delighted to, of course. Won't you come in?'

My visitor was aged about twenty, thin and angular. His hair was too long but he looked otherwise all right. Since it was impossible to stand upright in the tent unless you chanced to be a midget, and also because of my position on the ground, I was unable to judge his height. He wore a green plastic cape over his shoulders, tight trousers, orange socks, and silly little town shoes with pointed toes. He stood the lamp on a moderately raised part of the floor, squatted on his heels to see whom he was talking to, and laughed.

'What you need in here, pal, and no mistake, is a groundsheet.'

'So I am beginning to think. The water seems to be rising.'

'Reckon you don't do too bad rolled up in the sack. Right handy is that.'

'There's a zip which runs down the side. But forgive me if I don't get out: it's a great business getting in again.'

'Aye, like as not. I've come looking for my mate. Went for walk, like, and hasn't turned up.'

'You don't think perhaps he's drowned?'

'Never likely.' He laughed again. He was a jolly person, obviously thinking the situation was a huge joke. Life, in fact, a huge joke. 'Happen he hasn't shown up around here then?'

'There was someone a little while ago, but he didn't come in. As he didn't say anything I went to sleep.'

'Aye, that would be our Ron.'

He straightened up as far as the limits of the tent would allow and picked up the hurricane-lamp. His socks clashed painfully with the yellow canvas walls, but this was not his fault and I was sorry to see him leave.

'Cheerio,' he said.

'Cheerio,' I said. The word was not part of my vocabulary: it enlisted itself quite naturally.

An hour later I was making the first of the pack journeys back to the Abbey. It was barely dawn and the rain had stopped. The earth had an elemental smell about it, and, after its unaccustomed week of sun followed by the cloudburst, was making little bubbling noises of satisfaction, sighing and sucking, glad to be back in the Wales it

196

knew and far away from the Sahara. Steam rose from the ground so that the Abbey below, and the trees and roofs, were hidden. I was well in time for the morning office in the chapel, wondering as I found my place in the breviary whether Ron had turned up and how the two of them were going to manage for breakfast.

At my own breakfast later on there was a letter from a priest friend of mine, Father William Jolly, who had just bought a small sailing-boat and was anxious that I should join him for a voyage from East Anglia, where he was stationed, to Holland. Father Jolly is some ten years younger than I am, sharing my tastes exactly. His letter told of the great heat then enjoyed in East Anglia and reminded me of a walking tour which we had planned years ago but which for some reason had never come off. This proposed sailing expedition was meant to be a substitute for the Pyrennean venture discarded long ago.

Also among my letters that morning was a coloured folder, an advertisement from a firm with some such name as Happy Hiking Ltd or Cozycamp & Co which urged the holiday makers of Britain to 'trek the *thorough* way'. It showed collapsible canoes, collapsible cooking kits, collapsible chairs and tables, collapsible baths and beds. Even collapsible bicycles, and of course every possible kind of collapsible tent. (The more expensive tents were called 'canvas residential units'.) But I had had enough. There was still a collapsible tent waiting for me up on the hill which I would have to bring down some time.

In my reply to Father Jolly I explained that I was now too much of an old stay-at-home for his adventure. Years of sybaritic ease had left their mark. I wished him well on the enterprise, and hoped that when he reached my age he would be able to rough it with the best. For him there was still time, but as for me, if ever I should be up-rooted from Wales and felt ready again to travel, I would have to do it in comfort — on a raft in the Caribbean with Dr Sears.

STELLA

On the first day, more than a year ago now, she looked away, refusing to meet my eye. Next time she frowned. I didn't think I had
much chance but I don't give up easily. A week or two later when I
was again walking through that part of the property, which I have to
do if I want to get anywhere from the Abbey, she waved. Stella was
at that time just six years of age. Her parents are Welsh, poor, and of
humble stock. I'll come back to them in a minute. Stella is the only
child.

There are low walls where she plays, and trees with low branches,
but Stella seems to feel no urge to climb. Perhaps she has been told
not to. But I doubt if this would put her off. She tends to forget
instructions. My theory is that she is so busy remembering other
things that what her mother says simply slips off. Her mother can
hardly have told her not to run about, and she doesn't seem to do
much of this either. But perhaps it's the shoes she wears.

She sits for ages in the long grass. Sometimes she makes a pile of
the big stones which have come loose from the wall and sits on that.
Her toys are not the toys you buy in shops. She has two matchboxes
which she uses a good deal, and a variety of tins. Pieces of string have
constantly to be detached from one object and made into the harness
of another. My enquiries as to what function the boxes and lids
perform have met with no success, and perhaps this is because the
function is always changing. At least I imagine a matchbox is not
always a chariot or a car. It would be very dull if only its position
changed on the path or in the jungle of long grass. I can understand
that if you once tell a grown-up that a matchbox is an engine or a
steamroller you have more or less committed yourself. The grown-up
mind can't be expected to see how today's ambulance can be something quite different tomorrow.

Though she talks to me more now than she used to, and without
being prompted in the way of subjects, it can still be heavy going at

times. When she is in a bad mood, that is. She has her off days, silent days. This will be an obstacle later on. It's not my place to tell her. She doesn't smile enough either, but when she does it is good to watch. I have learned to tell the smile a long way off, the kind of smile it will be, rather as during the war one learned to tell the different aeroplanes. Most children's laugh — I have gone on from smiles to laughter now — is pretty well always ready, and is only accidentally related to something funny. Stella shows no sign of being amused unless she really *is* amused. It has taken me a long time to discover what things she thinks funny. I have got it now, but I do not use the formula often.

What usually works with children, I find, is a little gentle teasing. Not perhaps at the beginning, straight off, but when you have come to know their favourite phrases, their particular hates, their hobbies, They like you to laugh as long as you are laughing for their benefit and not for yours. As long as they can join in they don't mind being gently teased. It's just that they don't like being laughed at. I don't blame them. But this won't do with Stella. However gentle the mockery she shuts up like a clam.

One of the obstacles to conversation is not only her limited vocabulary but that unless I speak very slowly she cannot understand a word I say. If my accent bothers her, hers bothers me. The difference is that I'm quite ready to repeat my last remark, however inane, while if she says something I don't understand and I say 'What?' she either goes on to something else or remains silent until I have started another topic.

At first, because her reactions were slow, I thought she might be stupid. But when I heard her with other children I knew she was as bright as any of them. While the others babbled along in a way almost wholly unintelligible to me, Stella seemed to follow it, coming up with apparently appropriate responses. Nevertheless I noticed that when other children were present she let them do most of the talking. She would withdraw into some Welsh part of her which I knew I could never understand. All I could see was a rather vacant look. The Welsh are funny like that: they retreat for miles and for a time are lost to you. It would be a wearing experience to be on a desert island with a Welshman.

Anyway there she would be all by herself with the others lively as ping-pong balls. Deep thinking perhaps, but to me it looked sulky. You see I'm not claiming anything very wonderful for Stella. She isn't a remarkable child. Ordinary — if any child of six is that. What I'm trying to do is to give you something to go on for when I come to describe a particular occasion. But first the background must be filled in. The Welsh mother and father.

The mother is a lanky ungainly woman with a bad complexion and dry straight hair. She gives the impression of being a slattern, and to look at her leaning against the door of her cottage you would say she was lazy, but there always seems to be washing on the line and she can frequently be heard banging about the house with presumably a broom. Stella is clearly afraid of her. Who wouldn't be? She so far acknowledges my existence as to nod at me when she sees me, her invariable cigarette doing a slight bob of recognition. Stella told me once that her mother was glad when a stranger like me took her (Stella) off her (the mother's) hands. I could hardly picture the mother being glad about anything, but it was reassuring. She has not invited me in, but I suppose this is nothing unusual in Wales. She wears no stockings, winter or summer, and I have never seen her in a pair of shoes. Dirty pink slippers, with cream-coloured lining folded over the outside and cream-coloured pompoms dangling uncertainly, are evidently good for out of doors.

The father is a builder. At least this is what he is supposed to be. He is out of work a good deal because he drinks. I see him rarely, and he, too, nods when we meet. I was walking back from the bus-stop one evening and saw him sitting on the low wall between his cottage and the road. Without stopping to talk I said cheerfully that I had made friends with his daughter. All he said was 'Ar', and I saw he was drunk. Though neither he nor his wife is unfriendly, I have an idea neither of them likes Catholics. I have carefully avoided talking to Stella about religion.

But the Stella family must be familiar with Catholicism, because there's a Catholic household almost next door. The Dunns do not come to Mass much, and I have not yet discovered how many of them there are, but there is no doubting their nominal allegiance. One of them is called Timmy, who is often to be seen playing with Stella. Timmy is a year younger than Stella.

Timmy's mother rather gives herself airs. A cut above Stella's mother. She wears make-up, red trousers, a flowered print top as if hot from Hawaii's beaches, and white sandals. Despite all this dash, her hair is seldom out of curlers, and over the arrangement of cylinders and clips which looks like a crowded car park she wears a lemon-coloured plastic hood, which, being transparent, would seem to defeat its purpose. She too smokes incessantly, and is as talkative as Stella's mother is taciturn. She stops me in the village street to tell me about her clerical friends. Her priests are all canons or about to be canons. Some are monsignori. She knows all abut the nuns whom I serve here as chaplain, and gives me messages for them. They have never heard of her. She knows when the Bishop will be going to Lourdes. Endless church patter comes clicking out through her false teeth which are of the gentlest shade of blue, and at the end of every sentence she says 'father'. I can never understand why someone should want to be a walking *Catholic Herald* yet come to church only for Midnight Mass and Easter. Her husband, equally strong, it seems, in the faith, does not appear.

'Little Timmy's going to be a priest, father, so he says. Always putting up candles and that. Oh he's a one, I can tell you, all energy and go. A pity he can't give that poor Stella some of his spirit. Such a sour mite, Stella, and no wonder.'

'I have not found her sour.'

'Always brooding, father, and that sly look. Seems like she's afraid of people. I often say to Bert, my husband, how sad to see a child like a dog that's been whipped.'

'Aren't a lot of children silent at that age? Perhaps Stella is shyer than most. Your Timmy isn't shy.'

'It's the home, father, that's what it is. Timmy isn't shy, but then we're a happy family. But what's little Stella to go back to? Scrapping, scrapping, scrapping. And him as good as an alcoholic. It's not nice in front of a child, father, not that.'

I'm not sure that I like Timmy an awful lot. He talks too much. Also he's inclined to show off. It's not altogether his fault, it's partly his mother and partly television. He will suddenly break off a conversation, jump on to the wall I have mentioned, and with a heroic gesture cry out, 'Come on, fellers, let's go.' He's an extrovert, and probably finds people like Stella and me too slow for him.

Timmy, like his mother, addresses me as 'father'. At first this puzzled Stella. She had her own idea about fathers.

'Why you call him father,' she asked Timmy one day in front of me, 'he's not a father.'

'He's a priest. And all priests is father.'

'Silly,' said Stella, examining some petals which she had pressed into one of her matchboxes and which were already beginning to fade, 'silly.'

The question of calling me something must have been suggested by this exchange, because next time we met she asked me my name. Timmy wasn't present, and I doubt if she would have asked if he had been. I told her my name in full, as though I were answering a policeman, and it sounded very long. It must have sounded even longer to her.

'What's the real part?'

'The important part you mean? What is called the surname is the van Zeller part. But you don't have to remember that.'

'Ranzeller.'

'No, van Zeller. Say it after me: van Zeller.'

She repeated it until she had got it right. Next time we met she called me by it, and thereafter. I am now simply 'van Zeller' whether Timmy likes it or not. I am reminded that Turgenev makes the women in his novels address their lovers by their surnames. I must remember to notice what she calls the postman and the man who delivers the bread.

The postman seldom has occasion to stop at the Stella household, but the man who drives the bread van always has something to say to Stella. He is a pleasant young man, but makes the mistake of using baby talk. It embarrasses me to listen. It is like hearing a man tell a story to people who you know have heard it before. Stella looks away and stuffs her fists into the pockets of her pinafore.

'Well, isn't *that* a treat then?' cries the bread man with enormous zest, 'them pretty lids and bottles and all. And what does your dolly think about it I'd like to know.'

202

Enthusiasm unwarranted by the situation always makes me feel hot.

Timmy's enthusiasms are different. His sense of the dramatic may be tiresome but it makes up for what is lacking in situation. A great quality in Timmy is the ability to create his own world as he goes along. And if it is not Stella's world he doesn't mind.

One afternoon when we were talking, Stella and I, Timmy burst through the bushes turning his head from side to side as though pursued. Though it was a hot afternoon he was wearing his overcoat, and when he spoke it was in his hoarse television voice. Stella made no move. I obligingly took cover behind the tree-stumps on which I had been sitting. When Timmy judged that the last of the poisoned arrows had gone singing past our heads, we sat on the grass and I asked him why he was wearing his overcoat in the steaming jungle when the Brazilian summer was at its height.

'It's a secret,' he said, folding his arms over his chest as though I was going to strip him of his coat.

'You mean you're hiding plans to blow up the bridge? There's something in your overcoat pocket, Timmy, which Stella and I may not see?'

'It's not a secret like that,' said Timmy darkly, 'not one in a pocket. It's a secret I keep, like.'

'All the more reason to tell it,' I said, throwing moral principle to the winds. 'Come on, Timmy, be a sport.'

I knew he was longing to tell his secret and would be bitterly disappointed if we changed the subject.

'O.K. but don't tell anyone, mind. You first, Stella.' He held out his arm rigid in front of him so that the palm of his hand was within an inch of Stella's face. 'Smell,' he commanded.

Stella drew in a deep breath, wrinkled her nose, and breathed out again. She said nothing. It was my turn.

Squinting down the sleeve of Timmy's overcoat, and sniffing more broadly than Stella had done, I smelled hot young arm as might be expected, but also, and surprisingly, strawberries.

'Strawberries,' I said, and was glad to see that Stella nodded in agreement, 'but not fresh strawberries. What's the story, Timmy?'

'We went down to the beach Tuesday, see, and there was

strawberries because m'auntie was home and she give us all strawberries, three baskets. It was cold and I had on me coat while we was
eating these strawberries, and without my noticing I must of slipped
some up me arm and squashed them there. I didn't know it till
I was going to bed, and next morning the smell is still there, see?'

'And now you wear your coat whenever you can, is that it, so
as to remember the time on the beach?'

'Yar.'

'All you have to do is put your arm up to your face and sniff, and
nobody notices? Well, Timmy, I call that a pretty good idea. The
smell is still quite strong, and should last you a long time yet. But
isn't it sticky — squashed strawberry up against your skin?'

'Nice and cool.'

At Timmy and Stella's age it is normal to be sticky. It would not
be noticed any more than the smell of hot bare arm would be
noticed.

Stella looked at her own chubby brown arms, and I wondered if
she was wishing she had an overcoat with long sleeves and strawberries to squash in them.

This reminds me that I have not yet described her appearance
and dress. By no stretch of affection could she be called beautiful.
She has a comfortable round face like a bun, a bun which isn't
giving away a currant. Her reddish hair falls over her eyes in an
irregular fringe, and when the fringe grows too long and she wants
to look up from her seated position to a standing caller she parts
it as though drawing a curtain. This gesture makes me laugh every
time, and even Stella herself is beginning to think it funny. Sometimes she brushes her hair aside with whatever she is holding: a
wooden ladle or a broken wooden spade. Her mouth is small and
well shaped, and most of the time her lips are drawn in out of shy-
ness or concentration. When she looks down at the complexities of
her matchboxes, tins, and bottles a chubby roll of double chin
appears. Plump arms with dimples at the elbow, sturdy legs with
dirty knees, plentiful scabs and bruises.

The distinctive feature of her costume is a pair of spangled black
velvet shoes, sharply pointed and several sizes too big for her. The
heels make running almost impossible. I asked about these shoes

204

and was told they had belonged to her cousin Liz who works as a waitress in Rhyl. Liz is sixteen and, if the shoes are anything to go by, dressy. I gather that most of Stella's clothes are cast-offs. They are too big for her, making her look smaller than she is. Not long ago when I was passing the jungle of trees, bushes, ferns, weeds, and the small clearing where Stella and Timmy play — the plantation being only a few hundred yards from the yellow villa where I live — I heard Stella calling, 'Van Zeller, van Zeller, stop.' I stopped, and a moment later she appeared at the side of the road in a pink cotton dress with short sleeves and a red hem reaching to her knees. Hideous, but new. 'Look,' she said, and turned round so that I could see the back as well.

'My holy hat, Stella,' I cried, shaken our of my habitual calm, 'where on earth did you get that?'

'Liz give it. She done overtime.'

'Do you mean Liz *made* it? That bit at the back which ties up?'

'She earn overtime and buy it. It zips at the side, see, so the tie-up bow isn't real.'

Her eyes shone with a brightness I had not seen before, and when she pulled in her mouth so that the lips disappeared I hoped she was going to burst out laughing. She didn't laugh but looked down at the red trimming to her dress, and raised her arms to shoulder height to make the most of every visible inch. If she had not been wearing those preposterous shoes, she might have skipped. The dress, the present from cousin Liz with her overtime earnings at the cafe, must be only for special occasions. It has not appeared since.

The incident which I have taken such a long time to reach, and which took place quite lately, has to do with one of our rare Welsh heat waves. More accurately with the end of it. I had walked back from Prestatyn more quickly than usual, thinking a storm was on the way, when I was hailed to the patch of dry sun-baked grass on which Stella was sitting. She looked tired, yet when she talked she seemed to be excited.

'What's up?' I asked, 'aren't you feeling well?'

'Feel,' she said, dividing her fringe with her two hands.

I felt her forehead. It was warm and sticky.

'It's this funny weather,' I told her, 'and it's given you a headache.'

She turned her head right and left, and then shrugged her shoulders. It was as if she had tried to shake off the headache and then given up bothering.

'Haven't you ever had a headache before?'

'No. Will it stop soon?'

'Sure to. It's just waiting for the storm to break, and then it will go.'

As we were talking we heard the first drops of rain, and I thought we would get soaked. They came smacking the leaves and dappling the dry dust. But only a few of them. It was a false alarm.

It was enough however to bring Stella's mother to the door of the cottage.

'Come in out of that.' It was a harsh voice. Stella busied herself with collecting her belongings, which she put very carefully in a dirty cellophane bag, but she was not quick enough because the summons was repeated. I looked across the twenty yards or so which separated us at the sallow hard face of the woman in the doorway, and wondered at the uneven distribution of well-being in the world. I saw her stiffen, and it struck me that she was perhaps more angry with me than with Stella. But in fact it was neither of us which roused her this time: it was the sight of her husband weaving a not very direct course down the hill behind us. I felt suddenly sorry for her.

As I watched Stella toddling indoors with her headache and her cellophane bundle I felt the electricity in the air as if it had been turned on from a switch. It seemed to me that life was building up a bit too much for that family.

By the time I reached the priest's house the lull of silence was over and it was raining hard. There was still an hour before luncheon but I found I couldn't settle down to work. I was restless and depressed. An image which I could not get out of my mind was the back view of Stella, whose build should have made her look comic but who in fact looked infinitely pathetic, which told so much more than she would ever have been able to tell in words.

There was no thunder or lightning. The deluge rattled down in rods, but so far as my spirits were concerned it brought no relief. I began typing — always a distraction because I type unskilfully and if the result is to be legible I have to give my whole attention to the job — but before I had got half-way down the page I heard someone thumping on the front door. That it might be Stella did not immediately occur to me. She had never been to the house, and so far as I knew had no idea where I lived. It was when I heard the door being kicked by pointed shoes that the identity of my caller was made clear. *Stella tempestatis*. She was not big enough to reach the bell so was banging with all she had.

She was also crying. I had not seen her cry before, and the contorted childish face was a disturbing sight. I pulled her through the door out of the rain. Her wet hair, plastered against her head, dripped over her ears and neck and looked almost chestnut in colour. Her pinafore was soaked, her shoes were muddy, and she had left her cellophane bundle behind.

Squatting down on my heels I took both her hands in mine. She had not unclenched them since thumping on the door. They were like lumps of soft warm putty: little wet dumpling fists which I prized open gently with my fingers. Choking on her tears and heaving deep breaths which raised her from the waist upwards, she put her arms round my neck, and I felt the damp smelly little body clinging to me. 'Van Zeller, van Zeller,' she said in a hoarse whisper right up against my ear, 'it's me mum and dad.'